"If you've ever been caged by a lie, this book is for you. If you've ever run in circles after a falsehood, this book is for you. But if you've ever had the desire to break free and rise above—this book is most certainly for you."

Mark Batterson, *New York Times* bestselling author
of *The Circle Maker*; lead pastor of National Community Church

"I love how Clayton highlights the lies that are holding us back *and* equips us with truths to move forward. *Overcome* will empower you to break free from the devastating entanglements of the enemy!"

Lysa TerKeurst, *New York Times* bestselling author;
president of Proverbs 31 Ministries

"Reading *Overcome* is like walking up to a door, turning the knob, and entering a new world of hope, healing, and possibilities. You are going to love this book."

Derwin L. Gray, lead pastor of Transformation Church;
author of *Limitless Life: You Are More Than Your Past
When God Holds Your Future*

"Over the past few years of leading Catalyst, overcoming issues, lies, and barriers has become a central skill for me as a leader. During that time I've watched as Clayton has been doing that very same thing, with great success. I just wish he had written *Overcome* earlier so I would have had this amazing playbook to help me along the way!"

Tyler Reagin, executive director of Catalyst

"If you have experienced life for any time at all, then you know the battle that rages in our minds is very real. I am so thankful for Clayton, who has provided us with a biblical game plan to identify the lies we tell ourselves and a framework to process the toughest faith questions we face. This book is a brilliant resource that can lead us to life-changing breakthroughs *as we seek to renew our minds and become more like Christ.*"

Chris Brown, Ramsey Solutions

"*Overcome* is probably Clayton King's best book to date, and that's saying something. In it he plays the role of a spiritual counselor. He helps the reader identify the spiritual lies that have held us down and articulates the spiritual truths that liberate us from those lies and their devastating consequences. If you are a Christian who wants to live a freer and truer life, this is the book for you."

Bruce Ashford, provost and professor of theology and culture
at Southeastern Baptist Theological Seminary;
author of *Every Square Inch* and *One Nation Under God*

"Listen carefully to my friend Clayton King as you read his wonderfully written and practical book *Overcome*. It will help you overcome fears and misperceptions that afflict all of us as he deals with real-life issues punctuated by real-life examples. One of my favorite sections of the book discusses suffering. King says it well: 'If your suffering won't go away, it might as well go to work.' I love that! Listen to this and many other practical points that can help turn your life around and help you overcome!"

Dr. Frank S. Page, president and chief executive officer of the
Executive Committee of the Southern Baptist Convention

"Most people wouldn't dare walk into a UFC octagon and take on the world's toughest, meanest opponent. Yet every morning when you wake and your feet hit the floor, you've stepped into the cage fight of your life! It's the truth of who you are and where you're headed against the lies of what you aren't and where you'll never be! Clayton King's life bears the scars of a man who has taken on life's lies. His testimony is a trophy of victory. What are you waiting for? The bell has rung! The fight is on! Read *Overcome*; you'll tap into the power that will have lies tapping out!"

Tony Nolan, evangelist, author, and mentor

"We Christians all too often fall prey to 'axioms for living' disguised as reasonable presuppositions that could not be further from the truth. In this book, Clayton reveals them for what they are—deceptive lies—and points us to the truth and grace of Christ that challenge us to live instead by authentic faith."

Evans P. Whitaker, PhD, president of Anderson University

"I highly recommend reading *Overcome*. Clayton is a tremendously effective and authentic communicator of God's Word. We've all bought into the lies that have held us down, and as Clayton states, 'It's like chasing a unicorn.' *Overcome* is transparent and presented in a way that links us to the practical biblical truths that set us free. I have been blessed by reading it and know you will be too."

Bruce Frank, lead pastor of Biltmore Church

overcome

overcome

Replacing the Lies That Hold Us Down
with the Truths That Set Us Free

clayton king

BakerBooks

a division of Baker Publishing Group
Grand Rapids, Michigan

Published by Baker Books
a division of Baker Publishing Group
P.O. Box 6287, Grand Rapids, MI 49516-6287
www.bakerbooks.com

Printed in the United States of America

Library of Congress Cataloging-in-Publication Data is on file at the Library of
Congress, Washington, DC.

978-0-8010-1681-3

The author is represented by the FEDD Agency, Inc.

Some names and details have been changed to protect the
privacy of the individuals involved.

17 18 19 20 21 22 23   7 6 5 4 3 2 1

contents

I have told you these things, so that in me you may have peace. In this world you will have trouble. But take heart! I have OVERCOME the world.

John 16:33

foreword

J esus certainly didn't talk like an Overcomer.

Blessed are the poor in spirit, for theirs is the kingdom of heaven.

Blessed are the meek, for they shall inherit the earth.

Blessed are those who mourn, for they shall be comforted.

Blessed are you when others revile you and persecute you. Rejoice and be glad; your reward is great in heaven.

This, however, is the mystery of the gospel. The way up is the way down. The way to gain righteousness is to confess your unrighteousness. The way to grow strong is to admit your weakness. The way to become wise is to confess your foolishness. God only fills empty hands, and so only when you are weak in yourself can you be strong in him. Those who overcome the world are not strong themselves but strong in their confidence in God. That's what this book is about.

Therefore, this is not your typical book on how to meet and overcome life's challenges. It's not filled with trendy, never-before-heard life-coaching strategies. That's because this book is not really about *you* at all. It's a book about Jesus and how you can find victory above life's challenges by letting Jesus overcome them through you. Those who overcome are not those who do something *for* Jesus but those who let Jesus do something *through* them.

Clayton King is one of our generation's most effective communicators. His insight, grasp of Scripture, and wit know few rivals. These things, however, are not what make Clayton a great preacher, nor are they what make this a great book. Clayton is a man mighty in the gospel, strong in his weakness, and that comes through on every page of this book. It is raw, authentic, and faith-inspiring. This book will not leave you amazed by Clayton. You'll leave it amazed by Jesus. Nor will you put this book down overwhelmed by all the things you now need to do. You'll put it down overwhelmed with gratitude at what Jesus has done for you, and how—just as he has done amazing things through Clayton and his family—he can do them through you too.

I have had the privilege of calling Clayton King one of my best friends for more than twenty years now. His boldness and loyalty have always inspired me. I've seen him share the gospel when everyone around him kept their mouth shut, whether in a gas station in a small town, before groups of hostile high school students, or with gang members in South America. I don't know of a more powerful preacher. I've seen him stand by a friend's side when everyone else turned their back. He is a relentless believer in people and he refuses to give up on them. I don't have a more loyal friend—lots of things in the last two decades have changed in my life, but Clayton has remained constant. In relationships, life, and faith, he is an overcomer.

I think the reason I'm so excited about this book is that it shows you *why* Clayton is that way—the power behind the man.

I've heard the passion behind these messages and watched up close as they were lived out in real life. My humble (but entirely accurate) prediction is that you will be blessed by this book in ways you have by few others.

If you don't believe me, just read and see.

J. D. Greear,
founding pastor, The Summit Church;
author of *Jesus, Continued*

introduction

Confessions of a Sick Pastor

I hate being sick. Not because of the fever or chills or sore throat or stomachache. I hate being sick because it keeps me from working. I love to work. I'm good at it. It makes me feel alive.

I don't get sick very often, but when I do, I can trace my steps backward and see the pattern that led to it.

It usually goes something like this.

Sometime around the holidays, generally right after Christmas, I feel it coming on. My throat gets scratchy, I sense a fever brewing, and I start making my way toward the medicine cabinet to overdose on vitamins and zinc in an attempt to hold off the plague.

I wind up on the couch or the recliner in a gray haze of fever-induced sleeplessness and total loss of appetite. I get angry. I can't do anything. I have no energy. I want to see friends, get coffee, and have lunch with people because it's the holidays and things have slowed down for everyone. It's the one time of the year I have time to see people and I'm coughing up alien membranes all night long. And that's exactly why I get sick at the same time every year.

Here's what I mean.

For years I didn't see the progression. I would push myself for months and months. I would travel too much, preach too often, accept too many invitations, and fill my plate too full . . . because there was work to be done! Naturally, I would stop exercising regularly because I just "didn't have the time." This, in turn, would increase my stress levels and diminish my body's natural defenses. And we all know that when we are overloaded, it's harder to eat healthy and way easier to eat junk and fast food with lots of calories and little nutrition.

Additionally, because of the workload I willingly took on, my mind would begin spinning as soon as I would lie down to go to sleep at night. I couldn't turn it off. I would think about upcoming projects, sermons to write, book deadlines, staff meetings, fund-raisers, new hires. On the nights I could fall asleep without trouble, I would wake up between 2:00 and 3:00 with a compulsion to get up and work. Then I would be sleepy (and grumpy) the rest of that day.

This would go on for weeks every fall leading into the holidays. I couldn't rest, so my resistance was shot. The pattern repeated itself for several years, but I was too blind to see it. My wife, Sharie, saw it, though, like she sees everything. Thank God for her ability to notice what I miss.

It was the day after Christmas. I was storming through the house like a raging Brahma bull, complaining that "This happens to me every year," and "Getting sick ruins my Christmas," and "I don't get to see anybody or spend the holidays finally doing something I want to do. Why me? I am cursed! God is punishing me for something. Satan is attacking me!"

With great care for my soul, Sharie gently spoke up. "This is what happens to us every year. We go and go and go. We take on too much. We don't take time off regularly. You don't have a Sabbath day each week. We work too hard and say yes to too many things. We wear ourselves out telling ourselves that we will rest up during the holidays. But when the holidays get here, our bodies finally slow down enough to actually get sick. We need to listen to our bodies. If we want to get better, we have to change our pattern."

Sometimes I think my wife helped write the Bible.

The Lie That Lurks Beneath

It made perfect sense. She nailed it.

Now that I have seen the progression of how I get sick every year and am fully aware of the pattern I fall into, it's up to me to change the process. I can't blame it on anyone else.

Before I can deprogram my destructive pattern and reprogram a better perspective on work and rest, I have to dig down deep and recognize what is driving me to abuse my body and ignore reasonable limits on what I can accomplish. At the very bedrock level of this annual cycle of sickness was, and sometimes still is, a need to achieve. I am addicted to accomplishment.

At the center of the destructive pattern was a lie. And I wasn't just listening to this lie. I believed it, was controlled by it, and often didn't even recognize it as the cause of the havoc in my life.

The lie that fueled my sickness was the belief that I needed to do more in order to be more successful and thus more content:

more speaking opportunities, more people responding to the gospel, more ministry relationships established, more promotion for our camps and mission trips. For me, "more" was like a drug that gave me a sense of euphoria. It made me feel alive, important, valuable, and respected.

When I finally got what I thought I wanted, I realized I didn't want it after all.

I was chasing a unicorn. There would never be enough achievement to make me feel at peace. I would never have "enough" to make me really happy. Like a hamster on a wheel, I kept running and running but ended up in the same place: sick in bed every December, missing the fun and the joy and the people I was supposed to enjoy during the holidays, praying to get better so I could get back to work.

I believed the lie that if I worked harder I could achieve more, which in turn would make me feel more accomplished and respectable. The trap was hard to recognize, because hard work actually does pay off! But I was never happy when I reached the end goal. To put it bluntly, when I finally got what I thought I wanted, I realized I didn't want it after all.

The lie I believed was what I like to call a root lie, or a bedrock lie, and it led to my self-destructive behavior. I wasn't simply getting sick because I was worn out every Christmas; there was so much more lurking beneath the surface. The truth was, I thought that if I worked hard enough, people would notice and respect me, I would feel good, and God would love me more. I was blind to this pattern for years, and the lie was eating me alive.

I believe a bedrock lie lurks at the root of every unhealthy choice we make, every fear we allow to dominate us, and every dysfunctional pattern we cycle through over and over again.

If we can learn how to identify these bedrock lies, we can dig them out at their root and finally halt the cycle of bad choices and self-destructive behavior.

This, friends, is exactly what we are going to do in this book. In identifying and unpacking nine bedrock lies, we will overcome the questions and problems that have plagued us for ages and walk with new freedom into God's peace.

I want to expose the power of the lies we listen to. I want to show you how to *identify the lie* and *fight the lie*. I want you to overcome.

I won't preach at you. My heart is not to beat you down but to lift you up. If I can, I want to teach you some things I've learned through my own struggles, as well as the many things I'm still learning as I walk through hard times with those I love, as I read the stories of others who have been set free from the endless cycle of fear and anxiety, and as I listen to God whisper encouragement and truth to me as I grow and change. Thank you for trusting me enough to read what I have to say. I'm glad we can take this journey together.

Notice the Pattern

I've picked nine of the most common lies we believe. We will unpack each of them together, but first I want to show you the progression of how one tiny thought in our head can snowball into an avalanche of negativity and despair. The lies we listen to are leading us somewhere—and the destination is always destruction.

The truth takes you to a better place, but you'll never get there unless you learn to recognize the lies when you hear them. And we all hear them. All the time.

I've learned the quickest and most accurate way to tell the difference between a lie and the truth is to tune in to the way it makes me feel about myself, others, and God.

The lies we listen to are leading us somewhere—and the destination is always destruction.

A lie isolates me, accuses me, and condemns me. It makes me feel shame.

The truth challenges me, invites me, and liberates me. It makes me feel free.

This is always the pattern. If we can pay attention to the pattern of the lies we listen to, we can predict the process. We can prepare to find the lie and fight the lie.

Here's how lies work. If we believe lies long enough, they:

1. Infiltrate
2. Insinuate
3. Intimidate
4. Re-create

Watch, for example, how the lie of achievement and success played out for me.

First, the lie *infiltrated* my mind with subconscious thoughts: *You know that some of the biggest and best speaking opportunities of the year happen around the holidays. You might want to take them, because they may never ask you back if you say no this time. And just think of all the people who will get saved, or hear about Crossroads Summer Camps. Plus you're getting older and these events won't always be there for you to take. Take them now. You're tough and conditioned for it.* The infiltration is always subtle, like a stealth attack by mind-ninjas—so subtle we fall for it without putting up a fight.

Next the lie *insinuated* that if I said no, I was a bad husband and father and a spiritual wimp: *You could turn down these opportunities, and that would be okay because everyone needs time to unplug. But just know that if you do, they will call someone else. And they will think you're a diva who can't take the heat of ministry. They will probably talk about you to other churches and ministries and warn them not to call you. Or maybe not. But is that a chance you're willing to take? Remember, this is your calling and your source of income. This is how you provide for your family. You do love them, right?* The insinuation is that if I don't say yes, I'm a bad father and husband. And a spiritual weakling.

Then the lie *intimidated* me by making me feel like I don't really love Jesus or ministry: *Just think about all the other Christians around the world who suffer for Jesus every single day. They get locked up in prison and murdered in public because they won't stop preaching the gospel. And here you are, invited to preach the gospel to thousands of people, and they will fly you there on a plane and pay for your meals and hotel, and no one will be there with machetes or machine guns to stop you from preaching. But hey, stay home for a few days and rest if you need to. Just remember, you get paid a salary to do what other people die for.* The lie intimidates me by making me feel spiritually inferior to others. When I play the comparison game, I lose. Every time.

> If we can pay attention to the pattern of the lies we listen to, we can predict the process. We can prepare to find the lie and fight the lie.

Finally, the lie *re-created* my reality: *If you were a man of God, you wouldn't even hesitate to fly to Montana on Christmas Eve to preach at a candlelight service with thirteen people. So while you're spending time with your friends and family, reading your Bible and resting, you may want to ask God to forgive you for being so shallow. Actually, ask God if you're really even a Christian, because real followers of Jesus know there's work to be done now and they can rest when they're dead.* At this stage, I'm doubting my calling, my salvation, and whether or not I'm even going to heaven when I die. The lie re-creates my own identity and makes me feel ashamed and condemned for making a wise decision. If I listen to it long enough and let it get this far, the lie has already buried its tentacles into my mind.

> Once our eyes are opened to the pattern, we can predict the outcome and preempt the process.

Do you see the pattern in my situation? I believed the lie that I needed to achieve more to be happy, so my life spun out of control as I chased the false promise the lie dangled in front of me. It's the same progression each of us falls into, regardless of which lie we believe at any given time.

However, once our eyes are opened to the pattern, we can predict the outcome and preempt the process.

Fighting the Fight

By now you may assume that I've beaten this lie. You might think it's been years since I was sick during the holidays, that I've learned my lesson and have fortified my spiritual and emotional defenses to withstand not only this lie related to achievement and success but all the flaming lies hurled at me.

If only that were true. Sadly, I'm still a work in progress. Why do you think I'm writing this book?!

This book is for you but it's also for me. I'm preaching to myself as I reveal my scars to you. I'm telling myself the same things I'm sharing with you, because overcoming the lies that hold us down is a process that's never completely finished. It's a lifelong journey that requires daily attention.

I think of it like eating. I never have a meal and declare, "Well, that was delicious. I'm glad that's over. Eating can be quite a hassle and I've got other things to do, so let's get on with life." Eating is essential to living, so it's a daily part of the life I live.

Likewise, confronting and overcoming the bedrock lies that hold us back is essential to living (at least living a truer, freer life). It requires vigilance. It's never over. But it's for our good, and if we get in the habit of replacing lies with truth, the process becomes as second nature to us as eating.

As we spend some time together, I hope you will remain open to some new ideas about how you can overcome the lies that hold you down. I also pray you will invest the time to work through this now, because the sooner you learn how to shut down the lies and listen to truth, the sooner you can get on with living a freer, truer life. You can do this! You can overcome.

Now let's get started.

1

getting to know the real God

And Trusting Him with Our Wounds

> **THE LIE:** "God is mad at me, and that's why my life is filled with hurt and disappointment."
>
> **THE TRUTH:** God loves you more than words can express. He wants to heal you and make you whole.
>
> Who is it that OVERCOMES the world? Only the one who believes that Jesus is the Son of God.
>
> 1 John 5:5

had seen the look dozens of times over twenty-five years of ministry: anger, frustration, fatigue. She was a total stranger, but I didn't need to know her name to recognize the look. She was on a mission, like a guided missile released from its bunker to find the bull's-eye. And she was coming for me.

This happens a lot. I find myself in situations where confused and hurting people lock on to me after I preach, weapons fully loaded, looking for someone to unload on.

They're not mad at me. They're mad at God, and they're mad at God because they think God is mad at them.

Oftentimes, after I speak at a conference or preach at a church or college, I will spend an hour afterward in the lobby or foyer or even down front at the stage, meeting people and talking and listening to their stories. This is something that comes naturally to me as an extreme extrovert. By no means do I think every pastor or speaker should do what I do, but this helps me connect with people and see the real power of the gospel and the Word of God unleashed in their lives. It keeps me close to real people—their stories, their struggles, and their victories.

Yet this kind of approachability also leaves me wide open to hurting people with hard questions. In this particular case, I could read the hurt on her face as the woman hovered outside the crowd of people waiting to talk to me in the lobby.

As the people filed out one by one, I saw my chance. I stuck out my hand and introduced myself to this lady who had been waiting with a scowl on her face. "Hey, I'm Clayton," I said, a simple greeting that usually doesn't get me in too much trouble with most folks.

"Oh, I know who you are," she retorted. "I just listened to you preach. I've got some questions for you. I hope you're ready."

Wow. She didn't tell me her name or anything about herself. She simply announced her intentions. I could sense a deep pain inside this woman's heart. It was thick in her voice and it hung on her facial expression like heavy baggage.

She took the direct approach and didn't bother with subtlety. "You seem to be some kind of expert, so tell me . . . if God is so good, why has he treated me like *trash* all my life?" (The actual word she used was not "trash.")

She was mad. I half expected to see steam billowing from her nostrils.

Now imagine with me, for just a second, the sort of internalized tension she must have felt and the hard things she must have endured for her to:

- Blame God for all the negative, hurtful things in her life.
- Have the courage to approach me, a total stranger, and immediately take the conversation to that level of seriousness (and awkwardness).
- Skip right past all the basic manners and common courtesies afforded to most people upon first meeting them and dive headfirst into deep theological waters.

She was courageous. She had also reached a point of utter misery, and there's nothing like pain to motivate a person to take a big risk. She had long stopped caring about offending God or a minister like me. She wanted answers.

She had a story, like we all do, and she believed God was punishing her. It was God's fault her life had turned out differently than she had wanted it to.

I breathed a silent prayer, asking God to help me and give me patience and wisdom, and then I invited her to lay it all on the table: "Well, I can see that you're upset and you're hurting. I know there's a story there. Tell me what happened to you."

She didn't need me to ask her twice.

"I want someone to tell me why God is mad at me. I mean, I just want to know what I did to deserve everything that's happened to me." Her face contorted into what looked like agonizing disgust as she spewed these words.

"Why don't you tell me what happened to you?" I said.

"How much time do you have?" she asked.

"I want someone to tell me why God is mad at me. I mean, I just want to know what I did to deserve everything that's happened to me."

I honestly didn't have a lot. I had a plane to catch, and planes don't typically wait on passengers before they leave, but I wasn't going to tell her that. She was within striking distance of a major breakthrough, and I didn't want to discourage her from taking the plunge.

"Just go ahead and start talking. I'll tell you if I have to go, but right now your story is what matters most," I said. The look on her face changed, just enough for me to notice her exhale and relax a bit.

"Well, ever since I was old enough to remember, I've felt like God was mad at me. Everything in my life is so screwed up right now. And it's been that way since I was young, probably about twelve years old. My mom and dad fought all the time. I mean really fought. Like, screaming and cussing and throwing things at each other. Sometimes my dad would get so drunk he hit my mom. Like, really hard. He knocked her out a couple of times."

Then she paused. I think when she heard herself say it out loud, that her dad beat her mom in front of her, she realized it was the first time those words had ever left her mouth. It was as if she had suppressed the painful memory of seeing her father knock her mother unconscious.

While she took a deep breath, I took my cue. "Did he ever hit you?"

That simple question, five small words, cracked open a vault of feelings. The woman exploded into involuntary sobs, wailing, doubled over right there in the lobby in front of a dozen or more people. She wept and wept, crying, moaning, hands first covering her face then clutching her stomach.

When she finally composed herself enough to speak, she answered. "Yes, he hit me." And then (I am not embellishing) she started to cry again, but this time at twice the volume and force as before—loud wails of anguish. She sank to the floor, oblivious to those around her.

I was at a loss. I looked over to where some people were standing, and as soon as I made eye contact with them, two of the ladies immediately came over to us. They sat down beside the woman, put their arms around her, asked her name, told her who they were, and then started praying. They stayed with her for a few minutes, then they all stood together and hugged, mopping away the runny makeup and tears.

Then the woman, barely composed enough to force some words into a sentence, said to me, "I guess I just always thought God was mad at me because my daddy was always mad at me. I wondered what I had done that was so bad my daddy would beat me the way he did."

I wondered how long that burning question had been locked away in her wounded heart. "God is not mad at you," I replied. "God loves you, and he wants you to be healed and made whole. I think these two ladies were sent here to be God's hands and feet for you tonight."

The ironic thing about the experience is that I never got to hear her whole story. But in fact, she actually didn't need to tell me her whole story, even though that was her stated intention at the start. She instinctively knew she had to let go of the hurt that was poisoning her, but she couldn't predict how things would play out once she decided to open up. Obviously she didn't become instantly healthy after spending a few minutes talking to me and crying. She had a lot to overcome. Yet in those few minutes a shift had taken place, and she had changed direction.

She was equating her abusive, angry father with God, assuming that God was like her dad.

When she walked away from me with those two precious ladies, she took a step away from deception and destruction toward truth and healing.

The lie she believed was that God was mad at her. She was equating her abusive, angry father with God, assuming that God was like her dad.

The fear lurking beneath that lie was that her life would always be filled with hurt and disappointment.

The truth is, God loves her very, very much, and he was not the source of her anger or her brokenness.

It's easy, in hindsight, for you and me to read this woman's story and see exactly what she was doing—the lie she was believing and the fear beneath the lie. It's a lot more difficult, but much more important, to identify the lies and fears that cause us to misunderstand who God is in our own lives. That's what we're going to try to do in this chapter.

The Angry God

There's a deep, rich tapestry of religion woven into the fabric of American history. Our nation was founded by religious rebels—women and men who were determined to throw off the tyranny of rulers that restricted their religious freedom. As the age of exploration blossomed in Europe, people poured into seaports by the thousands, filling wooden ships to the brim, hungry souls longing for a new start in a new world where they could worship God as they chose. These rebels, who followed in the footsteps of Luther and Calvin and Zwingli, became known as "Protestants" because they protested against religious and political corruption that limited their religious liberty.

As a new world formed across the Atlantic, one man had a significant influence on the American Protestant movement. His name was Jonathan Edwards. The catalyst of Edwards's fame and influence, as well as the beginning of the Great Awakening, was a sermon he preached to a congregation of church folk in 1750 called "Sinners in the Hands of an Angry God."

As American literature and journalism were just beginning to find their footing, Edwards's sermon on the realities of God's judgment on sinners went viral before there was an internet— when "going viral" usually referred to things such as smallpox or influenza. Though it was preached to a relatively small congregation at Edwards's church in Massachusetts, the sermon itself took on a life and identity all its own. We would probably assume a sermon with a title like this would be a "hellfire and brimstone" lecture delivered at fever pitch with screaming and shouting at the audience. But upon examination of the evidence, it would appear that Edwards's message that day was delivered simply, directly, and void of theatrics.

Edwards's message came at a time when forces were converging and a new democracy began to bloom into what would become the United States of America. As one of my favorite writers, Malcolm Gladwell, would say, it was a "tipping point" of cultural, religious, and political forces coming together at just the right time and place. One sermon preached from a wooden lectern to a small congregation in New England would help frame how future generations would understand God.

So much of the current fabric of the American Protestant religion, including the way we look at God and the way we believe he looks at us, can be traced back, at least in part, to Edwards, his powerful influence, and this one sermon that lodged in the American psyche.

Perhaps we've adopted a Puritanical view of God that in some ways is true to his character in the Bible (including his hatred of sin, his demand for repentance, and his warning of eventual judgment on proud, unyielding sinners). Yet in other ways, the God who emerged from Edwards's sermon and the Puritan faith (the one that burned witches in the streets of Salem) looked more like an angry devil than the merciful Jesus we see in the Gospels.

Scripture refers to eternal punishment reserved for Satan, demons, and unrepentant sinners who refuse to surrender to Jesus Christ. It also teaches us that God is love and that love is the defining trait of his character. Jesus embodied this attribute as he faithfully loved sinners—prostitutes, tax collectors, lepers, and religious zealots—during his earthly ministry.

What's Your God Like?

So with this in mind, ask yourself what kind of God you believe in. When you hear the word *God*, what image comes to mind? The loving God you see in Jesus Christ, or the angry God who dangles sinners over the flames of hell by a thin thread? How you answer this question can help you understand in a deep and robust way how you relate to God and how you think he relates to you. As the great Christian writer A. W. Tozer once said, "What comes into our minds when we think about God is the most important thing about us."[1]

If we think God is mad at us, we will look at our self, other people, and life itself very, very differently than those who believe God loves them.

If we see God as essentially good, kind, merciful, and just, we will make certain assumptions about God and life (and the reason why certain things happen in our life) based on the identity we assign to him.

If we see God primarily as an angry, temperamental ogre, strictly enforcing rules for the sake of not being offended by worthless humans he created, this view will carry over into our daily life with a different set of internal consequences when we fail, mess up, or sin.

> *We tend to create an image of our heavenly Father based largely on our earthly father. This is a big deal.*

We tend to create an image of our heavenly Father based largely on our earthly father. This is a big deal.

The lie will look for a place to plant roots, and this could be fertile soil. Consider these examples, for instance:

- If your dad was demanding and harsh, you may think of God as impossible to please.
- If your dad was abusive, you may decide that you don't believe in God at all.
- If your father constantly screamed and lost his temper, you may be afraid that God will have an unpredictable outburst of frustration toward you every time you sin.
- If you never had a father or you had an absentee father, you might think of your heavenly Father as absent and uninterested in you.

Two Kinds of Dads

This is more than theory. This is reality. I saw it when Sharie and I began dating in the late 1990s.

Soon after we met and fell in love, we began to realize two things: we both loved God with all our hearts but we had very different ways of seeing God and relating to him as our heavenly Father, because we had different beliefs about how God felt about us and what he expected from us. These were largely based on our relationships with our earthly fathers.

My dad was not a perfect man by any stretch or standard. He was impatient, sometimes demanding, and occasionally prone to emotional outbursts. But overall my dad was a great man. He was my hero and my best friend. He was the single greatest influence on my life. He was my Sunday school teacher when I was a kid. He discipled me as a new Christian. He was faithful to my mom, provided for our family, cared for the poor, and practiced extreme generosity with those in our community and our family.

My dad was also an encourager. He used his words as weapons—weapons *against* discouragement and negativity. He bragged on his employees, complimented people in their work, and noticed small things and spoke up about them. Once I heard him tell a customer at his electric motor shop that the reason their business was doing so well was because of one employee who had a great work ethic. He said it in front of that employee, knowing he was facing a tough situation at home and understanding his words would lift the man up and give him something to hold on to.

My dad did this for me too. He was generous with his verbal affection and affirmation. I can still hear him cheering for me from the stands at my high school football games. He was constantly telling me how proud he was of me—when I made a good grade or a good tackle, or when I did a good job cutting the grass. Even when I messed up, he was still patting me on the back to tell me he loved me.

My concept of a daddy was a man who was kind, loving, firm, and faithful. I translated this into my concept of my heavenly Father. I had a good earthly father who loved me, so I thought of God as good and I knew he loved me.

Sharie did not have the same kind of experience with her dad or with men in general. Actually, she had multiple fathers and stepfathers. One of them was almost completely uninvolved in her life when she was a little girl and a teenager. He was a good man, but because he and her mom divorced when Sharie was very little, she never really knew him (more importantly, she never knew he loved her). It was only as an adult that she began to really understand him as a person and they were able to have a better relationship.

Sharie's concept of "father" was different than mine. She had only experienced pain and hurt from the men in her life. She never had real, meaningful conversations with her stepfathers. They never seemed interested in her as a little girl. She remembers feeling ignored, as if she didn't exist, because they seemed so distant and detached. She grew up thinking something was wrong with her. In her young mind she assumed she was the problem. She never knew a father's unconditional love.

Now imagine how that carried over to her concept of God. Even after she trusted Christ and became a Christian, it took years for her to deprogram from what she'd experienced and to reprogram a true view of God as a loving, trustworthy Father who would not use her or manipulate her or ignore her. She struggled to accept God as loving, kind, merciful, and trustworthy. Her broken paternal relationships led to a broken and incomplete understanding of her heavenly Father. That's not an easy thing to overcome.

I remember the first time I bought Sharie a gift when we were dating. I was so excited, and I waited until we were eating lunch one day at a Mexican restaurant to surprise her with it. But when I handed her the gift, the look on her face was not one of joy. Instead she looked tormented, like she was in physical pain. She seemed almost angry! When I asked her what was wrong, her response floored me. "Why would you give me something like this?" she asked me. "What do you want from me?"

I was dumbfounded. I stared at her for a second, my mouth gaping in disbelief. "What do you mean? I don't want anything from you," I told her when I could finally find my voice. "I love you and I want to give you something nice just because you're special to me. No expectations. No strings attached."

No kidding, right there in El Acapulco, Sharie broke down crying. These were not tears of joy. They were tears of confusion, of emotional torment, of a girl trying so hard to believe something good but only feeling something bad. That moment gave me a glimpse into the heart of the woman I was going to marry and spend my life with. She'd felt hurt, dismissed, and ignored by people who should have loved and protected her.

Finally Sharie composed herself enough to speak. "I'm sorry, I just have a hard time receiving anything good from anyone, because all my life, if anyone gave me anything, I always knew it was a trick to try and get something from me. Be patient with me, and I will do my best to believe that you really love me and are not mad at me or using me somehow."

That was a turning point in our relationship. The light came on for her, even if faintly, and she saw a glimmer of hope that not all men were absent or demanding or closed off. What had been broken in her young, tender heart—her inability to see God as loving and faithful—was about to be mended and made whole. Now, twenty years later, things are completely different. She knows I love her. She has seen a father who loves his kids (and hers) unconditionally. And she sees God as he really is, not through the lens of her "earthly fathers."

Sharie teaches, speaks, and writes books on this very issue. In retrospect, the way she *explains* what she went through is different than the way she *experienced* it. The way she processed it has given her perspective. And somehow God even used me in her life as an example of a good father. I learned from my own father, and he learned from God. God really is a good Father, but it takes time for some of us to see that as true.

Have you been looking at God through the lens of a lie?

So, again I ask you, how do you see God? What lens do you look through? When you think about him, does the image you have in your mind look like an angry, manipulative deity who's out to get something only for himself? Or do you see a God who is for you, who is on your side, who wants good things for you and takes delight in providing them? Do you need to overcome an incorrect perception of who God is?

Have you been looking at God through the lens of a lie?

God with Skin On

If you want to know what God is like and how he feels about you, you don't have to conjure an image in your head or consult dozens of experts to find out. You can go straight to the source for yourself and see him with your own two eyes. God actually

If you want to know the real God, you can find him in Jesus Christ, the epitome of self-giving, sacrificial love. showed us his face and revealed his character when he became one of us, lived among us, and proved once and for all that he can be known and trusted.

If you want to know the real God, you can find him in Jesus Christ, the epitome of self-giving, sacrificial love. The Bible is clear when it tells us that Jesus is God in the flesh, on a mission, sent by his Father for us.

Have the same mindset as Christ Jesus:

> Who being in very nature God,
>> did not consider equality with God something to be
>>> used to his own advantage;
>> rather, he made himself nothing
>>> by taking the very nature of a servant,
>>> being made in human likeness.
> And being found in appearance as a man,
>> he humbled himself
>> by becoming obedient to death—
>>> even death on a cross!

> Therefore God exalted him to the highest place
>> and gave him the name that is above every name,
> that at the name of Jesus every knee should bow,
>> in heaven and on earth and under the earth,
> and every tongue acknowledge that Jesus Christ is
>> Lord,
>> to the glory of God the Father. (Phil. 2:5–11)

If you've been living with the image of a cruel, vindictive God all your life, throw that image out and trade it in for the real God, revealed in Jesus. Jesus was sent by the Father to show us the

Father. Jesus said that he and the Father were one Person—that if we have seen him, we have seen his Father.

In John 1, we glimpse what was actually happening when, in the fullness of time, God decided that he would come and live among us for a short time:

> In the beginning was the Word, and the Word was with God, and the Word was God. He was with God in the beginning. . . . In him was life, and that life was the light of all mankind. The light shines in the darkness, and the darkness has not overcome it. . . . The Word became flesh and made his dwelling among us. We have seen his glory, the glory of the one and only Son, who came from the Father, full of grace and truth. (John 1:1–2, 4–5, 14)

For those who think God is only full of wrath and anger, you might be surprised when you read what Jesus actually said about God and his intentions toward us: "For God did not send his Son into the world to condemn the world, but to save the world through him" (3:17). God's purpose in sending Jesus was to rescue and save us. Does that sound like something God would do for you if he hated you? Or if he wanted to hurt you?

You may be wondering if God hates anything. Yes, he does. But not you. He hates sin. He hates rebellion. He hates pain and suffering. He hates all evil things that hurt his children, because he loves his children and he is holy. But he does not hate you. He is not mad at you. He has taken great steps to pursue you and save you.

Think, for a moment, about Jesus's final minutes on the cross. Luke, a medical doctor who investigated the life of Jesus and wrote down his findings in one of the Gospels, records that Jesus was crucified between two criminals. As the crowd taunted Jesus, one of the criminals joined in, mocking Jesus and challenging him to prove his power by saving the three of them from imminent death. Yet the other criminal had a completely different reaction to Jesus.

He actually defended him to the other criminal, admitting that they both deserved to be punished but that Jesus was innocent and didn't deserve to die. Then, in a last-minute request for mercy, he asked Jesus to remember him after they died and Jesus entered into his kingdom.

Not only did Jesus grant the criminal's request but he went above and beyond what the dying man asked for. The crucified man simply wanted Jesus to think about him when he got to heaven, but Jesus promised him that on that very day, he would grant him entrance into paradise. Or, to put it another way, once they died the undeserving man would open his eyes and realize he was in heaven. He'd never done a single thing to deserve that kind of grace. But he humbled himself enough to recognize his own need and Jesus's ability to meet that need. The love of Jesus was never displayed more clearly than at that moment.

Now imagine yourself in that story. See Jesus extending grace to you, offering mercy and love rather than anger or punishment. Replace the lie that God is mad at you with this image of grace, forgiveness, mercy, and, above all, love.

Stop-Sign Revelation

Both of our boys attended a Methodist preschool before they started elementary school, and I loved the time I got to spend with them in the car going to and from school whenever I was able to drive them. We laughed, made animal noises, concocted silly stories, and told absurd jokes. We also sang, usually at the top of our lungs. The song selection ranged from Thomas the Train to 80s pop to classic rock. What four-year-old can't use a little Def Leppard in his life? It was during these trips that Sharie and I also tried to instill in our sons the essential elements of God's story in history and the wonderful, good news of the gospel.

We told Bible stories about David and Samson and Moses and Noah. We also talked about Jesus and focused on his interactions with people, as well as his birth, crucifixion, and resurrection. My son Jacob really loved the stories of Peter walking on water and Jesus casting out demons. He would often interrupt me in the middle of my storytelling to finish the details for me. I loved every minute of it!

One morning I was teaching him a new song about the love of God that I'd learned as a small child in Sunday school. I'm pretty sure it's politically incorrect in our current culture, but I explained it to him and then began singing the words, "Jesus loves the little children, all the children of the world . . ."

A quick learner, Jacob immediately started trying to sing the words with me on my second pass. By the third chorus he was belting the lyrics like a pro, getting louder and louder with each word.

Then suddenly, as we pulled up to a stop sign on Highway 150, he cried out from the backseat with urgency, "Daddy, stop! Stop! Stop singing!"

I came to a complete stop and turned around in the driver's seat to see what was wrong. "What is it, Jacob? What's the matter?"

His answer has become one of those moments for me as a dad and a minister that's lodged a truth so deep in my heart I don't think I will ever lose it.

"Daddy, that song says that Jesus loves the little children. And I'm a little children. That means Jesus loves me!"

His eyes were as big as plates and he was pointing to himself, poking his heart over and over again with his finger. Then he clapped his hands together like he was applauding a great performance. And right there at a stop sign, my son got it for the first time. The love of God was not an abstract concept meant for other people. It was a real thing, and it was for him.

The love of God is a real thing, and it is for you.

That revelation alone is the single greatest thing that can ever happen to you. Maybe this chapter in this book is your stop sign, the place where God's love goes from abstract to concrete, from generic to specific, from a nice idea to a life-changing reality.

You can overcome the lie that God is mad at you. Replace it with the truth that God loves you and is for you. Trust Jesus when he says, "For God so loved the world that he gave his one and only Son, that whoever believes in him shall not perish but have eternal life" (John 3:16).

Next Steps

I'd like to lead you in a short but powerful exercise to help you focus on God's tangible, provable love for you. Grab a pen and prepare to search your memories.

Please list four tangible, specific ways that God has proven his love, care, and provision for you in your life. This short exercise will help you actually see some real ways God has come through for you, shutting down the lie that he is mad at you and elevating the truth that he loves you.

Here's an example from my own life: several years ago when we were moving to a new state, we desperately needed to sell our house.

After seven months of praying and waiting, God provided a buyer as well as a place to live in our new town, just in the nick of time, right before we moved.

Reflect back on your past for a few minutes, and then list four tangible ways God has demonstrated his very real love for you:

1. ....

....

....

....

2. ....

....

....

....

3. ....

....

....

....

4. ....

....

....

....

2

love and loneliness

Choosing Who Has Authority
in Our Emotional Lives

THE LIE: "I am unloved and alone."

THE TRUTH: God loves you the way you are, and he'd rather die than be without you.

What a person desires is unfailing love.

Proverbs 19:22

It happened again.

Boom. Like being blindsided by a freight train. It came out of nowhere and seized me by the throat. Pressure. Tighter and tighter. Then panic. And again, my body responded as if it was being attacked by a wild animal.

My heart rate spiked. My body temperature shot up, as evidenced by the sweat-soaked pillow and sheets. My ears were ringing like someone had fired an AK-47 beside my head. And my stomach . . . oh, my poor stomach. It was in knots, filled with hot anxiety from the dream I'd been captured in for only God knows how long. It could have been thirty seconds long. It could have been going on for thirty minutes. Or maybe it had been holding me captive for the last four hours, ever since I'd drifted off at 10:00 while my wife brushed her teeth in the bathroom just a few feet from our bed.

It didn't really matter.

What I did know was that I was now awake at 2:00 in the morning, startled by a power I couldn't control because it waited to attack until my brain and body were shut down. Well, at least my body was shut down. My brain was anything but.

At night, when I so desperately needed to rest, to catch a respite from the unpredictable circumstances of my life, my brain (evidently in an effort to sort out my myriad emotions, experiences, and memories) would kick into hyperdrive after I closed my eyes. And that's when the fireworks started.

Crazy scenes. Irrational scenarios. Some would call them bad dreams. Others refer to them as night terrors. Dreams so vivid that even inside the dream, I would ask myself if it was real or if I was dreaming. I would try to wake myself up and it wouldn't work, so I would resign myself to the fact that it was real. No need to try and leave. I was stuck. It was bad. This was my new reality. And this was before Leonardo DiCaprio freaked us all out on the big screen with a dream inside a dream, *Inception*-style.

I'm talking about a period of my life when, as a grown man, almost nightly I'd fall asleep only to be greeted by horrible, worst-case scenarios running rampant in my brain in constant, never-ending bad dreams.

In one of the dreams I preached a funeral and looked into the coffin to find myself staring back, face pasty and eyes half open. In another, my children careened over the edge of a gigantic waterfall in a canoe, the same waterfall that Boromir's dead body cascaded over in *The Lord of the Rings*.

One dream in particular revisited me again and again: my dad dying, screaming at the top of his lungs for me to help him, reaching for my hand and begging for me to come to him. As I would lunge for his hand, thrusting mine out to grab hold of his, I'd jolt awake, feeling like a stick of dynamite was exploding inside my chest.

It felt like madness. I was tormented by ceaseless dreams that wouldn't leave me alone. But the truth was, these dreams were simply symptoms of what was happening in my real, wide-awake world.

Several of my family members had passed away in a short time, and the nightmares were mirroring my life as it was happening. I was living through a season of tremendous loss. I was discouraged and depressed. Fear became my constant companion, anxiety my new normal. Things in my life were spiraling downward and I couldn't control them. The progression of my situation caused me to face some very hard realities.

I could not control anything.

I was a Christian, but God was not fixing things in my life.

I was physically tired and emotionally fatigued with no rest in sight.

I questioned why a pretty good guy like me would be suffering like this.

And here was the real kicker: I was about to become an orphan again.

Find the Lie

What caused me to experience hopelessness and depression? Why did I struggle to sleep, and what was the root of the bad dreams that startled, awakened me, and felt like someone had hit me with a cattle prod?

It was the knowledge that my very sick adoptive parents were dying.

That fact itself was not a lie. My parents were terminally ill, and the end was imminent. In the case of my father, it was about ten years from the time he became diabetic until he passed away. A decade is a long time to be sick. It's also a colossal amount of time to watch your dad go from big and strong to weak and frail. I had ten years to imagine his demise, a full decade to think about what life would be like when the man I loved more than life itself left this world and left me alone.

While it was true that my parents were going to die, the lie was much more subtle.

The lie was simply that when they died, I would be alone forever and no one would ever love me again. The fear that fueled the lie was my fear of being unloved.

Do you see it? How crafty and creative the lie can be!

My parents loved me unconditionally and faithfully. They were far from perfect, but I was blessed to be close to both of them. I grew up in a home filled with warmth, laughter, and friends. Almost every memory I have of my childhood and adolescence involving my parents is good.

I feared the death of my parents because of how it would affect me. I would be alone. I would struggle with my identity as an adopted son born to a fifteen-year-old teenage mother. I wouldn't know how to handle feeling like an orphan, with no parents or grandparents left before I turned forty years old. I would miss out on the joy of seeing my mom and dad love my own kids as they grew up.

I couldn't imagine living in the world without them.

The lie was that I would never be loved again. My fear was that I would be left alone. And that scared the life out of me.

Maybe you wrestle with this lie as well. Perhaps you have thoughts that reveal the real issue you fear—being alone and unloved.

What if my marriage ends in divorce like so many others?

If my family knew what I was struggling with privately, they would shun me.

People at school don't like hanging out with me because I'm no fun to be around.

What if I outlive all my siblings, my spouse, and my friends? I'll be all alone.

I don't know what I would ever do if I lost a child.

This is one of the major lies that humans have to fight. We are hardwired to love and be loved. We need people. They make us feel valued, cared for, safe, and needed. Naturally, we wonder what would happen if, for whatever reason, we didn't have people in our lives. But if we don't arrest that single thought and stop it from spinning out of control, it can turn into a vortex of despair in which we succumb to *If you can identify the lie and the fear that feeds the lie, you can be free.* the fear that eventually we'll be isolated from all meaningful human relationships.

How can you break free from the fear that you will one day be alone and unloved and the lie that it's inevitable? You face the fear and fast-forward to the end of it. Here's the truth: if you can identify the lie and the fear that feeds the lie, you can be free. You can overcome this lie.

Fast-Forward through the Fear

In order to not go totally nuts during that challenging season, I began meeting with a trusted Christian counselor. One day as I sat in his office, he probed down into a deep and frightened part of my soul. "What is it that you are really afraid of, Clayton?" he asked. It seemed like a silly question to me. I responded glibly, "I'm afraid my dad is going to die any day now." Like any good counselor, he knew when to draw back and when to push. This time he pushed.

"But Clayton, you already know your dad is going to die. He's been sick for years. And after losing your mom a year ago, you've dealt with the death of a parent. So this is not new. I think what you're afraid of is being alone and living in a world void of the love of your parents."

And just like that, the room began to spin. My forehead, back, and armpits began to sweat. The world changed for me right then and there. He'd nailed it. A direct hit to my heart laid me wide open to visceral, unfiltered truth. I was filled with understanding. Terrible, awful, liberating understanding. I had been believing a lie!

I would not be alone. I would still be loved. My wife and my children and my friends and my church were there for me, standing by me and showing me the grace of God. My parents were not the only people to ever love me. Ultimately I would always be loved by my heavenly Father. So why did I fear being alone and never being loved again?

Because I am human. And like all humans—like you—I find it easier to believe a lie instead of the truth. But just as light drives away the darkest of darkness, the smallest truth can immediately dispel the biggest lies.

My counselor followed up his mind-bending revelation with a series of questions that forced me to dive all the way to the bottom, to the bedrock of my fear. He was helping me dig out the root so I could overcome the power of the lie.

"So, Clayton, tell me what you'll do when you get the news that your dad is dead."

That was pretty straightforward. And macabre, and maybe even inappropriate. It was also a stupid question, if you ask me.

Just as light drives away the darkest of darkness, the smallest truth can immediately dispel the biggest lies.

"Well, I'm going to cry. And sob. And maybe fall on the floor and lay there in the fetal position." As if he didn't already know that.

"And then after that, what will you do?"

Interesting question. I had actually never thought that far ahead.

"I guess I will cry until I can't cry anymore, then I'll have to get up off the floor and pull myself together."

"And after you pull yourself together, what will you do?"

Now I could tell he was going somewhere with all of this. I didn't know where, but I would find out.

"I'll have to call a lot of people. My dad's brother and sister. My brother. My cousins. Maybe my wife and kids, if they're not there with me when he dies."

He just kept coming at me. "And what about after the phone calls?"

"Obviously, I'll have to make funeral arrangements. I'll have to close out all his accounts. I'll need to start the process of putting his estate into probate court. I'll have to get death certificates and call Social Security."

That had to be the last question. But no, this guy was a pro. "And after you make all those phone calls, what will you do then?"

"As much as I hate the thought of it, I'll have to go through his stuff. Clean out his house. Sort through his tools. The sooner the better, because I don't want to put that off. I'd like to get it over with. Then I'll put his house on the market." Good Lord, he had to be finished with these questions by now.

"And Clayton, after you've sold his house and kept the things that you want that belonged to him, what will you do then?"

It dawned on me. I thought I figured out what he was doing.

"At that point, I will move on with my life, I guess. Without my dad. I'll get back into a normal routine of being a husband and a father. I'll have forgotten what that's like, because it will have been so long. I'll grieve and cry a lot, but I think I will feel better with the pressure of caring for my dad and taking care of his farm while he was in a nursing home removed from my shoulders." And as those words rolled off my tongue, I felt like a monster-sized backpack filled with hot liquid lead rolled off my back.

The counselor had forced me to fast-forward through all the potentially gut-wrenching emotions I would go through after the death of my father. I was able to move those future fears from a purgatory of endless anxiety into the realm of concrete reality. I had never thought that far ahead. I always imagined my father passing away and then immediately falling to pieces like an incoherent, brokenhearted emotional mess. But I had never anticipated moving beyond that point.

It was strange for me to think about everything I would have to do once the big fear became a reality, and how forward progress through all the stages of losing my father would eventually get me back to living—as a husband to my wife, as a leader to our ministry, and as a father to my own kids.

My counselor forced me to play it out to the end, to fast-forward through the fear. I imagined what it would be like to overcome all that was still in front of me.

Once I faced those fears, I realized they could be overcome and that they would not ruin my life. I knew it would be difficult, for sure. But I also knew I could make it.

I was able to move those future fears from a purgatory of endless anxiety into the realm of concrete reality.

My father's death would mark me and it would change me, but it wouldn't be the end of me. When I emerged on the other side of the grief and loss, my scars would tell the story of what I had gone through and who I had become in the process.

The little exercise that day in my counselor's office was a sort of purging process. I exorcised the scariest scenarios from my mind. They had dominated me long enough. Like rehearsing lines before a play or an instrument before a recital or plays before a game, I walked through what I would do when the time came and I actually had to do it.

The time did eventually come, and it was anything but easy. Was I prepared for it? Did I crush fear and avoid grief? No, not exactly. I wept and screamed and hurt and hyperventilated. I fell down on my hands and knees beside my father's lifeless body in the hospice facility and cried until I was dehydrated. But at least I had experienced a run-through, a rehearsal if you will, before the real event took place. Playing it out to the end helped more than I can tell you.

The Way Out

I had a revelation. What I was actually afraid of was not my father dying but rather being alone and unloved. That lie held me down, and I would have to overcome it. It consumed my energy and made me paranoid. It caused me to be afraid to receive love and support from those who cared about me because I didn't believe it would last. I was afraid I would lose it—and lose them.

This is how you break free from the power of the lie. This is how you overcome. When you identify the lie and the fear that fuels it, your life moves from black and white to color. Or perhaps a better way to put it is that your life transforms from flat to three-dimensional. I began to notice the good things I had overlooked. The pressure I was under had blinded me to the abundant love that surrounded me on every side. My wonderful wife had been standing by me for years, supporting me and helping me through my parents' sicknesses, their surgeries, their recoveries in the hospital, and ultimately their deaths. She never complained but instead did whatever needed to be done. What a saint—and I was married to her!

When you identify the lie and the fear that fuels it, your life moves from black and white to color.

My own two children were a true gift of God's grace to me in that season. Many times my boys prayed for me. If they found me crying (which I did all the time), they spoke gently to me and then laid their hands on my shoulders and prayed out loud for Jesus to help me feel better. They went with me to see my dad before he died, visits which became progressively more draining and difficult as his health deteriorated. My sons asked me to tell them stories about their grandfather, which was part of the grieving process for me. They simply loved and supported me.

I also had so many friends who prayed for me, called to check on me, asked how I was doing, and sent me encouraging notes, emails, and texts. Immersed in the lie that I would be alone and unloved for the rest of my life, I'd missed all that love and support from all those people.

This is why it is so important to look for the lie that is holding you down. Cut straight to the source of the fear you're feeling and then ruthlessly cut it out of your life by replacing it with the truth. The lie has been robbing you of joy. It's kept you in chains.

How about You?

If you feel like you are alone and unloved, you're certainly not the only one.

You may be a college student who hasn't had a date in ages while all your friends are going out on the weekends. You may be a divorced middle-aged woman who feels like you've missed your best years and no man will ever show interest in you again. You may be a teenager who just wants attention and affection from your parents who are so busy with work they don't seem to ever notice you. Or you may be a single guy who feels insecure about your body, your income, and your people skills, and you think no woman will ever find you attractive.

The lie that you will be alone and unloved can come at you from every angle. Each of us is vulnerable to it. We feel it when we see big families together at restaurants and immediately feel sad that we didn't have a big happy family growing up. It attacks you when you see a mom or dad holding a precious newborn baby and you're still reeling from the miscarriage. It comes on strong when you see pictures of people you know posted on Facebook or Instagram at a party having a good time, and you weren't invited.

This is the critical moment to seize the crazy thoughts banging on the door of your brain. If you can stop the thought right then and there, and choose to refuse to be taken hostage by the lie that you are alone and unloved, it's a game-changer. Like deciding whether or not to go right or left on the interstate, the direction you take in that moment will determine your emotional destination.

How do you override the feelings of loneliness when the fear of being abused again is too strong to push through? Or how do you find the courage to initiate new friendships when you're still feeling rejected by old friends who never call, never come by, and never initiate intimacy with you anymore? Furthermore, how can you expect to trust someone enough to let them see the real you when every time you've ever done that, you've ended up regretting it? Can you really overcome the power of this lie and the fear it generates in you?

The answer may surprise you.

Receive the Love You Already Have

Sociologists tell us that our own self-esteem is not primarily based on how we objectively feel about ourselves. Instead, it is largely constructed from what we think the most important person in our life thinks about us.

In essence, there is a person (or people) in your life whose love and approval is so important to you, their perceived opinion of you is the single most powerful influence over how you view yourself and your value in this world. If you think they love and approve of you, you feel secure and valuable. But if you convince yourself that they don't like you or don't even notice you, you will feel invisible and unvalued regardless of how many other people do indeed care about you.

What if you changed who "they" is? What if you replaced the most important person in your life and their opinion of you with God and his opinion of you? What if he became that "most important person"?

This is how you break free from the lie that you will be un-loved and alone. You remove the person(s) from that primary place of authority and you place God there, choosing to base your identity and value as a person on what he thinks and feels about you instead of anyone else's opinion.

When we do that, it's more than a game-changer. It's a life-changer. Instead of constantly wondering whether or not you are performing well enough to elicit love, you can live in confidence that you never have to perform in order to receive love again.

Rather than living in constant fear of someone withholding love from you when you don't measure up, you can relax as you recognize that God never does this because he never requires you to measure up to anything. Instead of incessantly schem-ing ways to impress and please people in order to keep them in your life, you are liberated by the revelation that God is never impressed with anything you do and he never asks you to even try.

Listen, I am a dad. I love both my boys. I don't love them because they're perfect, because they perform, or because they offer me something of value. I love them because that is what a dad does. If that's true for me, a flawed human being, think how true it is of God.

God is our heavenly Father, and it's his nature to love his kids. So you've got nothing to prove and nothing to fear. You are not alone. You are not unloved. God is with you and he is for you. He showed how much he loved you when he sent his Son to die on the cross to take away your sins and rise from the dead to give you new life. That isn't just cheap talk and lip service. When God says that he loves you, he backs it up. He'd rather die than be without you.

You don't have to fear being unloved because you are already (and always) loved by God. No one to impress. Nothing to prove. Nothing to fear.

Replace the lie with the truth. You don't have to fear being unloved because you are already (and always) loved by God. No one to impress. Nothing to prove. Nothing to fear. Let that love redefine you and free you from insecurity, doubt, and uncertainty. You already have the most perfect, faithful love you could ever imagine. Open your eyes and see it. Open your heart and believe it. Open your hands and grab hold of it. Believe that truth. God loves you, and he will never leave you.

God doesn't love you because you're good. He loves you because he's good and he's God. That's what God does. He loves unconditionally and irreversibly. Knowing, believing, and remembering that is the way forward through the fear of being unloved and the lie that you will always be alone.

Push through the lie that fuels the fear by making God that "most important person" in your heart. You choose who has emotional authority in your life, and when you choose God, the lies lose their power.

This is how you overcome.

Next Steps

Let's put the principles of this chapter into action. Let's empower you to fast-forward through your own fear that you're unloved and alone.

Instead of avoiding the fear that no one will ever love you or pretending that you're really not afraid of having no close friends, go ahead and acknowledge that fear with courage. Write down your fears or even say them out loud. Exposing your fears to the light is the first step.

Here are a few examples to get you started.

I find myself wanting to ask people to lunch, but I chicken out because I don't want them to turn me down.

I'm afraid to go on an actual date because it may not go well and he may not like me.

I dread thinking about the next ten years because I know I'll be taking care of my aging parents who will eventually die and leave me alone.

One divorce has ruined my self-esteem, and I'd rather be alone than risk getting hurt again.

Next, face whatever fear of loneliness you've been carrying around and drag it into the open. Fast-forward all the way through that lie and feel how much stronger the truth is.

I've spent all my time wondering what other people think about me, but I know what God thinks about me. He loves me and wants a relationship with me.

I can't predict who I will date or who I'm going to marry, but I can count on God's unfailing care and provision in my life.

I have friends who invest in me, a family who loves me and would do anything for me, and a God who will always be with me. I won't be alone.

Everyone else is just as insecure and imperfect as I am, so if I keep that in mind, it takes the pressure off all my relationships. Because God accepts me, I have nothing to prove and nobody to impress.

These are just a few examples to illustrate how this personal exercise works. As you begin this new discipline, you'll find yourself feeling more and more liberated to be transparent and vulnerable with both God and yourself. You'll also likely discover that the effects of this practice will impact your relationships. You'll become less guarded, more confident in who you are, and more likely to give and receive the love that you were so afraid you would never experience.

3

reaching out to God

He Is Our Hope When
All Hope Seems Lost

THE LIE: "It's hopeless; things will never get better."

THE TRUTH: Nothing is impossible with God. Reach out and grab on to him when your life spins out of control. He will show you the truth.

> You, dear children, are from God and have OVERCOME them, because the one who is in you is greater than the one who is in the world.
>
> 1 John 4:4

Late one night, after we had tucked our boys into bed, Sharie and I were just about to drift off to sleep when we heard our four-year-old, Jacob, crying in his room. Jacob was going through a new and peculiar stage, one that amused me but disturbed my wife. It seemed he was on a mission to destroy everything in his sight. He pushed and hit walls, chairs, tables, and appliances. He repeatedly opened and slammed doors. He walked through the house screaming and would growl at strangers in the grocery store and in restaurants. In short, Jacob seemed to be producing way too much testosterone for a toddler.

Sharie worried that he was possessed or, at the very least, negatively impacted by too much sugar or too much Barney. Our conversations went back and forth, again and again—she would ask me if I thought our child was destined to be a criminal, and I would reassure her that Jacob's behavior was normal (though I did wonder if he might grow up to become a pro wrestler).

The night he awakened crying, I went into his room to find Jacob lying on his back, visibly upset, the covers pulled up around his face.

"Son, what's wrong? Did you have a bad dream? Daddy's here, and everything's going to be okay," I assured him.

"No it's not, Daddy. Everything's *not* going to be okay!" Jacob answered with emotion and conviction, not only rejecting my attempts to comfort him but also clearly disagreeing with me.

"What do you mean, Jacob? What are you talking about? Everything will be okay, I promise," I reiterated.

"No it won't, Daddy," my son insisted. "I'm so little. And I've always been little. Ever since I was born. And I don't like it. I want to be big and strong like you and like Spider-Man. But I will never be big! I won't ever grow up! I just want to be strong and awesome, but I will always be this small!"

Jacob then took his hands out from under the covers and held them approximately six inches away from each other, like he was showing me the size of a fish he'd caught. His response was both pitiful and precious. Jacob was convinced he would always be just six inches big.

It turns out Jacob's loud outbursts, incessant kicking and pushing, and intimidating growls at strangers in Walmart were all attempts to make himself feel bigger in a threatening, overwhelming world. His pediatrician later assured us our son's behavior was normal. As the human brain develops, our self-awareness increases, causing us to better understand our place in the world. As a kid I remember feeling like a little person surrounded by giants, and I'm sure you felt that way too. Our brains are hardwired to aspire to bigger, better versions of ourselves, which is why Jacob was so unraveled. He was upset because he didn't really believe things would get better for him. He believed he would always be stuck in the current version of himself.

Jacob's thought process was stuck in the spin cycle.

The Spin Cycle

I learned how to wash my own clothes in high school. I played football and needed clean practice clothes every day, so my mom passed that chore on to me. It wasn't until I was in college a few years later, though, that I really came to understand how a washing machine works.

One day, when I decided I couldn't wait until fall break to bring my dirty laundry home, I hauled a giant bag of dingy clothes and a pocketful of quarters up the street to the Laundromat. I loaded the machine, pushed the buttons, and sat down on a bench to wait. The washer was a front loader, not a top loader like my mom's, and the door was clear glass, so I could actually see the washing machine at work. I sat there mesmerized, fixated on the circular motion, the water and suds and clothes spinning and spinning, around and around. I was glued to it, sucked in, like the Millennium Falcon into the Death Star's tractor beam. The spin cycle had me locked down.

This is exactly how our mind works at times. We load our dirty laundry (our thoughts) into the machine (our mind). Stress, worry, and anxiety are the triggers, like pushing the buttons that start the cycle. Our thoughts get trapped in our head, agitating back and forth, spinning around and around in a seemingly never-ending cycle. Ultimately, we conclude that the frustrating, challenging situation we find ourselves in will never get better.

This is exactly where my son Jacob found himself the night he awoke crying in bed, terrified and convinced he'd be small forever. And this is exactly where many of us find ourselves too: stuck in an agitated, relentless thought process, convinced that nothing will ever change.

At times we all feel trapped inside the current version of ourselves, and we don't like it one bit. We want to change— to be bigger or better, healthier or stronger, more patient or less paranoid—but we succumb to an overpowering fear and negativity that convinces us change is impossible. Some of us give up fighting and submit to the belief that this is as good as it's ever going to get. We surrender to an enemy that's never even fired a shot at us. We're overcome by voices that fill our heads with lies.

Perhaps some of these internal "spin cycle" conversations sound familiar:

Because I haven't had a date in eight months, I might as well get used to being single for the rest of my life.

I never finished college, so I can't ever hope for a better job. I've hit the career ceiling and I will always make $31,000 a year.

My husband just has an anger problem. It's that simple. He only hits me occasionally, and at my age it's better to just tough it out than tell someone or leave him.

I've been depressed since I was a teenager. This is just how I am. I'll be this way until I die. I'll live with it.

Look at me. Past my prime and damaged goods. No one will be interested in a divorced forty-five-year-old man. From now on, the best I'll ever do is a one-night stand.

I'm thirty pounds overweight and my blood sugar is way up. I hope I don't get diabetes. But at my age, I just can't get in shape. There's just too much going on.

I feel ugly and ashamed because of my sexual past. I wish I could go back and change things, but I can't. I'll just always feel lonely and unattractive.

It's too hard to make friends. People are so selfish anyway. I've reached out, but no one ever invites me to do stuff. I'll make it on my own somehow.

These are just a few examples of the internal conversations we have with ourselves. I know you have these kinds of cyclical doomsday thoughts, because I have them too. Almost daily. Sometimes hourly. Mine sound like this:

I bet one of my kids will grow up to be a homeless drug addict. I mean, I have two, so odds are at least 50/50 that one of them will be a crack addict living under a bridge.

I'm aging out of ministry. People are going to stop calling any day now. Nobody wants a guy in his mid-forties preaching at their church or college or conference. I'm washed up.

I bet I have all kinds of diseases in my body. Since I'm adopted, there's no telling what I'm predisposed to. Hammer

toe. Japanese encephalitis. Whooping cough. Black lung.
Boils. I should find my birth parents and have some tests run.

We'll be totally broke when we are old. I know I started saving
for retirement when I was twenty-six, but when the market
crashes again (and it will!), we're going to lose it all. I hope
our kids will take care of us.

Our ministry is going to implode. My staff is going to turn on
me and run me off, or everyone is going to quit (on the same
day) and go start another ministry just like ours, in the same
city, but without me.

I wonder if I have cancer right now. I mean, I could and not
even know it. I could be a dead man walking. I probably
won't see fifty.

Sharie is going to leave me. I'm going to come home from the
gym one day and she will be gone. For good. Regardless of the
past eighteen years, and how faithful and godly she's always
been, she'll get tired of me and leave. Completely against her
character. But she will.

The pattern plays out as usual. These lies *infiltrate* my mind
without me even knowing it, *insinuating* that things in my life
will never get better, *intimidating* me into believing I just need
to accept reality, and *re-creating* my outlook and attitude to a
blind acceptance of a future that looks like a scorched post-
apocalyptic world with nothing but zombies from *The Walking
Dead* left on earth. If I let the lies take me down this familiar
road, I stop believing that God can help me change or that he
can change my situation at all.

When I read my list, part of me thinks I am nuts. None of
these scenarios are remotely true, yet I wind up worrying about

them as if they are inevitable. I am overcome. Sometimes I get so caught up in the relentless spin cycle of my internal thoughts, I manage to convince myself they represent reality. Before I know it, I find myself panicked over what to do with my son who needs to go to rehab for meth—my son who is ten years old, in fourth grade, and clearly *not* a meth addict. This is the insidious nature of the spin cycle.

My internal "spin cycle" conversations all sound like a version of the same lie: *things will never get better.* And like all other lies, this one is rooted in fear. We are afraid of stagnating. We are afraid we will never have the opportunity to move forward into a better life and the best version of ourselves.

Regardless of what your own personal spin cycle is right now, one thing is clear: it has to stop. The good news is that there is a way out; there is a way to stop the seemingly end-less spin cycle, and it's the same way you stop your laundry from spinning.

You overcome when you open the door.

Open the Door

We all want to stop believing that things will never get better, but how do we actually push the "off" button and stop going round and round? We open the door on our spinning, cycling thoughts and we call it what it is. In other words, we identify the lie.

Oftentimes, the lie that things will never get better is based on some element of truth. You may have a track record that supports this to an extent. Maybe it's been years since you went to church, so it's easy to believe that you'll never find a good one. Or perhaps you've been sick for weeks, so it's hard to think that one day you will feel better. Or maybe you've had serious problems with your family for so long you've abandoned hope that you'll ever reconcile or find a way to get along.

When these thoughts run through your mind, recognize them for how insane they really are. Then stop thinking them! Say it out loud if you have to: "That is a lie. I know it's not true and it's never going to happen. Stop thinking it right now." You may have to say it out loud more than once. Maybe dozens of times.

Also, remember that some lies are not as easy to identify. They're harder to discern because they masquerade as the truth, and it's tricky to tell the difference. This is where we have to lean on the Holy Spirit, who speaks to us in our soul (I like to call it "my gut"); the Word of God, which is the ultimate standard by which we gauge the truth and validity of any thought; and the wisdom and discernment of trusted friends who love Jesus and have insights that can help guide us.

Next, bring the lie into the open, into the light of day, so it can't run around in the dark like a crazy little cockroach in your head. This is precisely where the community of faith can be an invaluable source of clarity for you. Whether it's our pastor, sister, trusted friend, or mentor, it's remarkable how clearly someone from the outside can see the truth of our situation when we are blinded by lies and fear. You might also want to consider writing the lie down, maybe in a personal journal, a random notebook you keep by your bed, an app on your phone, or a few thoughts scribbled on the back of a Home Depot receipt. Whatever it takes to open that door and stop the spinning, do it. Confide in someone you trust; write it down and then put it aside. You will be amazed at how bringing the lie into the open can change your perspective.

Next, replace the lie with the truth, beginning with a prayer to God. It's not enough to talk only to yourself. Remember, your "self" is the one who sometimes feels crazy and believes the worst-case scenarios. You need someone else to extract you from the quagmire of yourself, and that's where Jesus comes in. Prayer is more than an item to check off your daily to-do list. It's a necessity for survival.

When I feel like things will never get better, I pray something like this: "Jesus, I don't want to stay stuck here. My mind is telling me that things will never get better, but I know that you love me. Your Word tells me that you died to save me. Please help me not believe these lies. Please fill me with your Spirit. Give me confidence that you are greater and stronger than what I am feeling right now. I choose to put my trust in you and what you say about me. I'm moving forward through this fear by faith in you."

In a very real sense, prayer alleviates the pressure we feel to solve all of our problems and puts that pressure on God.

Not only does prayer help you break the "spin cycle" thought process but it also connects you with Jesus in a real and tangible way. Prayer makes God the center of your thoughts, turning your vision away from yourself and toward him. In a very real sense, prayer alleviates the pressure we feel to solve all of our problems and puts that pressure on God. He is more than capable of handling the problems we face. Our problems don't crush God like they crush us. He has unlimited power to help us and an endless supply of care and attention to offer us when we are stuck in the swamp of self-pity.

Reach Out to Jesus

Remember earlier when I talked about lies that are based on an element of truth? The Gospel of Mark offers one such example—the story of a woman desperate for healing from a condition that had plagued her for twelve years.

Jesus had just crossed the Sea of Galilee and was on his way to heal the dying daughter of a local religious leader. But before he reached the little girl's bedside, he was distracted by the presence of another distraught and desperate person. Here's what happened next:

> And a woman was there who had been subject to bleeding for twelve years. She had suffered a great deal under the care of many doctors and had spent all she had, yet instead of getting better she grew worse. When she heard about Jesus, she came up behind him in the crowd and touched his cloak, because she thought, "If I just touch his clothes, I will be healed." Immediately her bleeding stopped and she felt in her body that she was freed from her suffering.
>
> At once Jesus realized that power had gone out from him. He turned around in the crowd and asked, "Who touched my clothes?"
>
> "You see the people crowding against you," his disciples answered, "and yet you can ask, 'Who touched me?'"
>
> But Jesus kept looking around to see who had done it. Then the woman, knowing what had happened to her, came and fell at his feet and, trembling with fear, told him the whole truth. He said to her, "Daughter, your faith has healed you. Go in peace and be freed from your suffering." (Mark 5:25–34)

This woman had been bleeding for twelve years.

Twelve years—the amount of time we typically spend in elementary and secondary school, from first grade through high school graduation. Imagine suffering relentless bleeding from the day you entered elementary school, all the way through junior high, and up until your senior year, to the very day you received your high school diploma. Imagine how embarrassing it would be to suffer from something so relentless and out of control. Imagine how desperately you would desire a cure.

Twelve years. That's how long this poor woman had suffered. That's how long her situation had remained unchanged. Do you think she ever lost hope? Do you think she ever concluded that her situation would never get better?

Consider also that she was most likely a Jew living in Israel among other Jews in a Jewish region. As a Jew, she was aware of the rules governing all things Jewish, rules that all revolved around being holy and *clean*. Out of the more than six hundred rules and regulations derived from the original Ten Commandments given by God to Moses on Mount Sinai, one had existed for more than one thousand years: the law that dictated proper protocol for a menstruating woman. Because blood was so precious and powerful in the sacrificial system followed by temple law, it was treated with great care. Considered unclean, a menstruating woman was isolated in an area outside the camp, excluded from community life until her cycle was over and she had purified herself. She was literally marginalized because of her bleeding.

We don't know the specifics of this woman's physical problem. It could have been hemophilia, or a bleeding ulcer, or a chronic nosebleed. But it doesn't require a medical degree from Duke to understand the impact of bleeding for more than a decade.

Once, back when I was in high school, I participated in a blood drive, mostly because I got to miss an entire class period. After I gave blood, the nurse instructed me to eat the cookies and drink the orange juice provided in the library. It was my first time giving blood and because I was a stubborn teenager (and an idiot), I refused the food. I woke up an hour later on a couch in the library as the nurse smiled and explained to me what blood does for the body and why I had passed out. Bleeding causes weakness and lack of energy. If you've lost blood, you can't do anything that requires exertion or extended effort. You feel exhausted after even the slightest amount of work.

This woman was more than weak. She was also poor—completely broke. As the text tells us, "She had spent everything she had" trying to get well. She had spent all of her money on various doctors and treatments, and not only had she not been healed but she had "suffered greatly" under their treatment, ending up worse off than ever. I imagine that all her friends and family gave her the name of every doctor and specialist around. Free medical advice, old home remedies, and strange rituals with weird ingredients were doled out to her like manna to the wandering children of Israel in the desert—but nothing worked.

Her body weak and her pockets empty, her soul weary and her reputation tarnished, this woman was undoubtedly ashamed and full of sorrow and despair. After suffering a dozen years, she must have thought to herself, *Things will never get better. This is how it is and I need to live with it. It will never change.* And yet she pushed through to Jesus in spite of her physical weakness and her emotional fragility. She reached out in faith to touch him.

Faith Fights Fear

After despairing for so long, we often resign ourselves to what we conclude is our "forever reality." It's often easier to accept our current circumstances than it is to hope for, or work for, a change. But in our resignation, we leave Jesus out of the equation. We don't ever imagine that he might be able to help us or that he may help us in a way we have never imagined or prayed for.

Think about the woman in Mark's Gospel again, for a moment. It's not unreasonable to assume this woman, most likely a Jew, would have prayed to God every day for twelve years, asking to be healed. If she prayed just once a day for twelve years, she would have asked God to change her situation 4,380 times. I wonder, have you ever prayed for anything that many times? Have I? Probably not. We usually give up after a few weeks if we don't see results.

This woman's persistence is breathtaking. The crowds pushed toward Jesus, everyone wanting something from him. Not surprisingly, a religious leader from the synagogue got to Jesus ahead of her. What's new? Religious people almost always got the perks in that culture. She was used to being overlooked and overrun. Yet she didn't give up. She persevered, pressing closer to Jesus. Perhaps she had to crawl to get ahold of him. She didn't care about getting dirty. She was already unclean.

How much faith did it take for her to fight the crowd and push through the morass just to touch Jesus's clothes? While it may have been a slight brush or a faint touch, I like to think of her grabbing hold, clutching his cloak, taking his garment in her hand and holding on to it for dear life, trying to wring the power from it like squeezing water from a dishcloth. I am reminded of Jacob, who wrestled with God all night long and said to him, "I will not let you go until you bless me."

She touched him, and instantly Jesus's power infused her with healing. She knew it, and he knew it, too, as he felt his power leave his body. So why did Jesus ask who had touched him? Of course he already knew. He is God, which means by definition he is all-powerful and all-knowing.

His disciples scoffed at the question in disbelief—how could anyone know who had touched him, with the crowd pressing in on them from all sides? What a silly question! But Jesus asked in order to showcase the woman's situation and her faith—to prove that he alone can change unchangeable outcomes, and to ensure that her story was recorded that day and passed down for millennia to come. Here we are, two thousand years later, still talking about the woman who reached out to touch Jesus's cloak. A nameless woman in a no-name region of a backwater Roman colony had the courage that only comes from utter desperation to reach out her hand to God.

Everyone was touching Jesus, but she touched him in faith. She grabbed hold of Jesus with a faith that fought through fear.

In answer to his question, the woman came forward, fell on her face before Jesus, and told him the whole truth. Everyone was touching Jesus, but she touched him in faith. She grabbed hold of Jesus with a faith that fought through fear. She believed that a touch would suffice. No need for words, or begging, or sacrificing; she simply wanted to touch him because she believed it would be enough.

The crazy thing is, she was absolutely right. She was healed. The bleeding stopped. Her shame vanished and her strength returned. And her story remains an encouragement to us, a reminder to reach out in faith toward Jesus when all hope seems lost.

Don't Give Up, Don't Let Go

The truth is, there will undoubtedly come a time in your life when you face a situation you absolutely, unequivocally cannot change. Maybe you're there right now.

Your credit card bill is astronomical. You will have to file for bankruptcy if they don't reduce or consolidate your debt.

You cheated on your wife. She caught you. You're so busted you can't even concoct a lie. And she will never trust you again. It's over.

You've been hiding your porn addiction from your parents. It consumes your thoughts day and night. You cling to your phone like it's your life, and you lie to your teachers, telling them you have to go to the bathroom just so you can catch another glimpse of a tantalizing sex act between people you don't even know.

You bought way more house than you can afford, and now you found out you're unexpectedly pregnant with your third child. You just went back to work after five years at home with your first two, and the double income allows you to make the mortgage, but just barely. You will lose the house if you can't sell it fast. And you haven't told your husband about the pregnancy test yet.

You've thought it through. You've written it out. You've Googled it. Heck, you even Yahooed it, just in case. But there is no solution in sight. Things will never get better. All hope is lost, and you know how things are going to turn out. No sense in wishful thinking. Go ahead and face reality. It will always be this way and there is nothing you can do about it. You can't overcome this.

Except for this: you can fight your way toward Someone who *can* do something about your desperate circumstances. And then you can grab him and hold on to him until he does, actually and definitively, do something about it. This is the way out. This is how you halt the spin cycle. This is how you overcome the lie that things will never get better. Grab on to God and don't let go.

Next Steps

Let's get practical, because what you really need now is to put a stop to the lies that perpetuate your own personal "spin cycle." Here are some questions to consider and action steps to take that will help you begin to move in the right direction.

1. What area of your life causes you the most anxiety and worry right now?

   ....

   ....

   ....

   ....

2. What issue or problem do you spend most of your time thinking about on a daily basis? Get specific, even if it's several things that are all connected in some way.

   ....

   ....

   ....

   ....

3. Is there a conflict, or maybe a tough conversation, that needs to happen with someone that you are avoiding?

   ....

   ....

   ....

   ....

4. Is there an unconfessed sin causing you shame or anxiety that you need to bring before God or another person so that you can experience reconciliation and forgiveness?

....

....

....

....

Now, here are some tangible exercises that will help you redirect your thoughts away from the spin cycle of lies and get you centered on the truth.

1. Write down your greatest fears in the space below or in a journal, then speak them out loud, both to yourself and God. In doing so, you disarm the lie of the fear it uses to hold you down.

....

....

....

....

2. Pray a simple prayer of confession to God, admitting that you are afraid and have difficulty breaking free from the negative thought patterns that have become ingrained in your mind.

....

....

....

....

3. Remember and recite specific instances in which God has answered your prayers in the past, protected you from harm, or come through for you (you might want to refer to the list you

made at the end of chapter 1). Ask God to repeat himself and help you reach out to him for healing from negative thought patterns.

....

....

....

....

4. Share this exercise with a trusted Christian friend, beginning with your struggle with your thoughts and moving through the process of writing it down, confessing it to God, and receiving his help in liberating you from the power of the lie. Then ask your confidante to speak into your situation with discernment and wisdom. Listen to him or her with humility.

....

....

....

....

4

understanding the purpose of suffering

God Uses Our Pain to Transform Us and Others

THE LIE: "Good people don't suffer."

THE TRUTH: All people suffer because we live in a broken world, but our pain has a greater purpose in God.

In some ways, suffering ceases to be suffering at the moment it finds a meaning.

Victor Frankl, Holocaust survivor

The light shines in the darkness, and the darkness has NOT OVERCOME it.

John 1:5

During the years I knew him as pastor of my church, Wilkes Skinner always seemed to be caught in the crosshairs of a major tragedy.

His oldest daughter was born with severe physical, mental, and emotional developmental disabilities, forcing Pastor Skinner and his wife, Mary, to place her in an assisted living facility for children who required round-the-clock specialized care. They would have rather raised their daughter at home, but they simply could not risk the potential dangers. Yet they loved her, spent time with her consistently, and never complained. I never once heard Wilkes or Mary ask why God had allowed their daughter to be born disabled. They were living examples of faithful people who trusted God in the midst of daunting family struggles.

Years later, Mary broke her leg in a skiing accident. The X-rays revealed not only the break but also that she was suffering from potentially life-threatening cancer in her bone marrow. The only hope for survival was a bone marrow transplant, a painful and long treatment that took over a year at that time. Mary and Wilkes moved from South Carolina to Seattle, Washington, where they lived for twelve months during her cancer treatment. Every Sunday morning before he preached, our church's interim pastor played a cassette tape for our congregation, a short message Wilkes had recorded and mailed across the country to our church. Our faithful pastor was still ministering to his flock from afar.

God spared Mary's life, and eventually she was able to come home, but she battled a case of shingles for many years after the transplant. She was in constant pain yet she never once complained. She still taught Sunday school and vacation Bible school and sang in the choir every Sunday. And she still continued to visit their daughter. Together, the family endured.

But perhaps the most tragic event to touch my pastor and his family was the death of his youngest son, who was killed by an automobile while playing in his own yard. I still get a lump in my throat when I think about the dark days their family walked through in the wake of that terrible tragedy.

The suffering Wilkes and his family endured didn't make sense. After all, he was a pastor, and God was supposed to take care of pastors. Pastors were good people who used to be bad people, and they were called by God to help a lot of bad people become good people, I reasoned. As I witnessed a good man, my childhood pastor, endure some really bad things, serious questions began to emerge in my young mind.

When I get to heaven, I want to ask Jesus why some people seem to suffer all their lives. It's an emotional question, I know, but truthfully, I've never been fully able to make sense of why good people suffer. This chapter is my attempt to wrestle through that question. If you've ever struggled with this, you've certainly asked the same hard question too.

Is Anyone Really Good?

An obvious answer to the question, "Why do good people suffer?" is that none of us is really good. In one sense, this is biblically accurate and true. The Bible is clear on this; in our own weakness, apart from the saving grace of Jesus Christ, we are completely void of any merit or goodness in and of ourselves.

As it is written,

> "There is no one righteous, not even one;
> there is no one who understands;
> there is no one who seeks God.

All have turned away,
    they have together become worthless;
there is no one who does good,
    not even one." (Rom 3:10–12)

The author of these words is Paul, the great pastor/church planter/theologian/evangelist who was converted by Christ from persecutor to preacher. He is quoting here from various Old Testament passages to prove to his Jewish and Gentile friends (who would read his letter once it arrived in Rome) that none of them was good without God. Of all people, Paul knew this to be true. He had climbed the ladder of personal accomplishment in the Jewish religious system. He was meticulous in following the law and all of its codes and expectations. Yet in his zeal to be a good Jew, he became so obsessed with achieving "goodness" he turned into a self-righteous persecutor of his own fellow countrymen, having them arrested and even killed for converting to Christianity. He knew the bankruptcy of trying to be good without God.

> *Each of us must depend on the goodness of God to make us good, to raise us from the grave of our sin into a new life found only in Christ.*

Make no mistake, no one is innately or inherently good. In that sense, there really are no good people. Each of us must depend on the goodness of God to make us good, to raise us from the grave of our sin into a new life found only in Christ. The goodness of God is what we call *grace*.

Paul had failed in his attempt to become a good person by keeping all the rules. He explains:

Therefore no one will be declared righteous in God's sight by the works of the law; rather, through the law we become conscious

82

of our sin. But now apart from the law the righteousness of God has been made known, to which the Law and the Prophets testify. This righteousness is given through faith in Jesus Christ to all who believe. There is no difference between Jew and Gentile, for all have sinned and fall short of the glory of God, and all are justified freely by his grace through the redemption that came by Christ Jesus. (vv. 20–24)

What Paul is saying is both simple and profound. All those who try to be good on their own, earning their own righteousness by observing the law and behaving well, will find themselves frustrated, falling, and failing. God, however, provides a way for each of us to be made new, to be raised from spiritual death, and he does it apart from the law and our attempts at performance and perfection. He offers this to us free of charge if we put our full trust in him and believe that he alone can save and sustain us. This is how we are "justified freely by his grace." It is his grace that makes us good.

And this is where things change. This is where we go from death to life. We go from cursed to blessed. We go from sinner to saint. We go from bad to good.

Once we put our faith totally and conclusively in Jesus, he makes us new from the inside out: "Therefore, if anyone is in Christ, the new creation has come: The old has gone, the new is here!" (2 Cor. 5:17). This is the only way anyone ever becomes a good person. Only through God. Only by grace.

So, yes, there are indeed good people: those who have repented of their sin, trusted God's provision for their salvation, and fully believed in him as their Savior and treasure are indeed made righteous and good by faith.

Which brings us back to my original question. If there are indeed good people, why do good people suffer? What about the Christians who have put their full trust in Jesus and yet still suffer? What about people like Wilkes Skinner? And what about the good people you've seen suffer?

Weakness and Witness

God works in our weakness because our weakness is our witness to the world. This is what I repeated to myself when I was going through the darkest season of my life. In other words, it's not our strength that makes people curious about our faith. It's how we react in our weakness that makes people pay attention. That is what drew my eyes and my heart to my pastor as a kid. I was an eyewitness to a good man enduring terrible tragedy, and I watched him suffer and survive.

I will never fully understand how Pastor Skinner was able to continue in ministry after suffering such unspeakable sorrows. But maybe God used those very sorrows to make him the kind of caring shepherd his sheep needed. He served the church in the midst of death, loss, and grief. He lived the life of Christ even while death raged around him. He lost nearly everything yet possessed a peace and joy that magnified the glory of God.

As a pastor who cared for the souls of people, Wilkes Skinner could never be accused of not understanding their loss, heartache, disappointment, or confusion. He had been where they were. He had suffered greatly. He was able to speak life and give life because of the loss and death that had touched his own. He could look into the eyes of a hurting family and say, "I understand."

The tragedies Wilkes endured were no secret and neither were the pain and suffering that accompanied them. I recall being amazed, as a young boy, at his ability to preach on Sundays when his wife was so sick at home. An unseen power both energized and sustained him in those dark and difficult days. He had entered into an intimate and personal place with Jesus Christ, a place I don't think I have ever been, simply because he had so much in common with Jesus in the sufferings they shared.

Pastor Skinner had no idea a little boy was watching him suffer. I had no idea God was allowing me the honor of watching a great man of God endure unspeakable pain and loss. I also didn't realize the experience would mark me so deeply and make me so different.

At age fourteen, I repented of my sin and trusted Christ. I immediately felt a call to ministry, and guess who was right there to encourage me? My pastor, Wilkes Skinner, of course. The first message I ever preached was from his pulpit on March 27, 1987. He told me I had an open invitation to preach any time I wanted, and after every one of my sermons he encouraged me and offered ideas for how I could improve as a preacher. A few years later, my childhood friend Brian also surrendered to the ministry. Wilkes treated him the same way and gave him opportunities to preach as well.

Wilkes and Mary are now with the Lord, but their legacy continues to live on in those who witnessed their faithfulness. Now grown men and best friends, Brian and I share a common denominator: the life and example of our suffering and faithful pastor. Brian is faithfully preaching the gospel to this day and is one of the most anointed evangelists I've ever heard preach. He has three sons and a daughter, whom he and his wife are raising to be world-changers for Christ. He is still one of my closest and most trusted friends, and has been faithful to God's calling on his life since he was sixteen years old.

I've preached in thirty-eight countries and forty-five states to several million people, have written fourteen books, and am a pastor at one of the largest churches in America. I am married to the loveliest, most Christlike woman I've ever known. Wilkes Skinner took both Brian and me under his wing and mentored us for ministry, and we are doing our best to model the endurance and faithfulness we saw exemplified in front of us.

A few years ago, Brian and I stood together on the Acropolis in Athens, Greece, and gazed at Mars Hill, where Paul preached the gospel to the Areopagus in the book of Acts. As we reflected on our lives and our callings and the power of the gospel to change lives, nations, and history, guess who we talked about? Wilkes Skinner. The man who stood strong even when death raged around him. The pastor who preached a simple gospel message and shepherded his flock with compassion. The man who opened his pulpit to two teenage boys and said we could preach anytime we had a message from God.

We asked each other what it was about Wilkes that had made him so special, and why he had continued to impact both of us so deeply even decades after we had moved away and moved on in ministry. The answer was clear. Without a doubt, it was the depth of suffering he had endured in life and his steadfast faithfulness in the face of all the unanswered questions, disappointments, and discouragement. Our lives would have turned out much differently had it not been for Wilkes. We would have never had that example of quiet confidence in God if he had not gone through all of the pain and loss he had endured.

God in his sovereignty used every bit of Pastor Skinner's suffering for another purpose. Long after his death, his life lives on. We were watching him. He was faithful. He overcame. He suffered greatly, and if ever there was a good man on this earth, it was him. His weakness was his witness, and I was a witness to that weakness.

Good People Do Suffer

The lie that we all want to believe goes like this: *Good people don't suffer. At least they shouldn't. Good people deserve a good life.*

I think I'm a pretty good person, especially compared to really bad people. So since I'm good, I shouldn't suffer. I deserve a fairly easy life.

Of course, no one ever actually says those things out loud, but many of us quietly and subconsciously assume them. If good people don't suffer, and I'm a good person, then I shouldn't suffer. And all the good people I know shouldn't suffer, either.

Yet we know this is simply not true. The truth is, good people suffer all the time, right alongside everyone else. No doubt, you have examples of people in your own family who were living for Christ when the bottom fell out of their lives. You could probably even tell your own story of a time when, in spite of being surrendered to Christ, your dreams were dashed, your heart was broken, tragedy struck, or a string of terrible events unfurled in a short time span.

My story is no different. I was baptized into the cold waters of suffering at the age of eighteen.

After I converted to faith at age fourteen, I was almost immediately flooded with opportunities to speak, teach, preach, and share my testimony. It seemed like a dream. All I wanted to do from the very moment I became a Christian was to tell everyone how God had changed my life. I prayed on my knees beside my bed every morning and every night, asking God to allow me to spend the rest of my life preaching the gospel and witnessing people putting their faith in Jesus. God answered that prayer. Local pastors invited me to preach in their churches. Youth pastors asked me to speak to their students. I even began to teach at a weekly service in a local prison facility before I was old enough to get my driver's license.

I had the complete support of my parents, my pastor, and my local church. I was seeing the fruit of my labors too. People responded to the gospel when I preached! It was more than I ever imagined . . . for about three years. Then my life took a turn for the worse during my senior year of high school.

First, my dad (who had worked for thirty years to build his own successful business) told us he might have to declare bankruptcy. The business he'd created was in trouble. He shut down for several weeks, laid off his employees, and tried to figure out a way to survive.

Next, I got bad news from my doctor about my shoulder. I had planned to go to college on a football scholarship. Football was the only way I could afford a college education, and I thought I was good enough to play at the college level. The football scholarship was my ticket out of my small town. Nearly a dozen small colleges were recruiting me to play for them, but when I informed them of my shoulder injury and impending surgery, their pursuit of me cooled. It looked like my football career was done.

Finally, just before Christmas, not long after my dad temporarily closed his business and around the same time I was forced to tell my coaches about my ruined shoulder, my mom had a severe stroke.

What was supposed to be one of the best seasons of my life blew up in my face like I had stepped on an emotional land mine. While all my friends spent their Christmas break planning what college they would attend or finalizing their scholarship applications, I cried myself to sleep, wondering if my mom would recover, if my dad would have a job after the holidays, and if I would even be able to attend college.

Is this really how things are supposed to go down? I thought to myself. *Has God forgotten about me?* After all, I wasn't the typical eighteen-year-old. I was preaching every week, leading a Bible study for prison inmates, and leading a prayer group that met every morning at our school. I even carried my Bible with me to class—every . . . single . . . class! On top of all that, I was still a virgin, and as captain of the football team I was pretty proud of myself for that accomplishment.

> *What was supposed to be one of the best seasons of my life blew up in my face like I had stepped on an emotional land mine.*

In other words, I thought I was a pretty good guy who had earned God's grace.

The lie I told myself, the lie that had settled into the inner recesses of my mind, was this: I was a good guy who had tried really hard to live a moral life in the face of temptation, and I had succeeded. I wasn't getting drunk or high or sleeping around like so many other teenagers at my school. Therefore, God owed me blessings, rewards, and protection from the kind of terrible things that happen to "sinners" who don't follow God.

The lie *infiltrated* my mind by *insinuating* that because I was a good Christian, bad things were never supposed to happen to me. Then it *intimidated* me into wondering what big sin I'd committed to bring on the suffering I was experiencing. It *re-created* my perspective about God when I became angry at him, blaming him for all the terrible things happening around me. I'd been overcome.

I'd become proud. I'd forgotten I was still a "sinner." I'd lost sight of the fact that I was just as undeserving of God's love and grace as the people around me. I didn't understand (at least not yet) that my good behavior and faith in Jesus did not insulate me from the pain of living in a broken world, a world where people have strokes and businesses close and scholarships evaporate.

> *I begged Jesus to show me what to do. Instead, he showed me who he was.*

I was getting an education, but it wasn't from a professor in a college classroom. I was sitting at the feet of a Jewish carpenter who had personally experienced the kind of pain, suffering, and betrayal I would never know. Jesus was teaching me that "good people" who have been saved by grace suffer just as deeply and just as frequently as "bad people" who don't yet know the grace and forgiveness of God. Jesus was showing me wonderful, terrible, unforgettable things in my dark season. Loss and fear of the future made me desperate. I begged Jesus to show me what to do. Instead, he showed me who he was.

Our Pain Has a Greater Purpose

I believe there is a side to suffering we miss when we focus solely on our pain rather than on God's greater purpose. If you can see the purpose behind the pain, you can find the way out of this lie. If you can see the purpose beyond the pain, you will understand God's ability to leverage the suffering in your life for greater things.

If your suffering won't go away, it might as well go to work. Hard times have the capacity to deepen your faith and the faith of those around you. And when you submit your situation to God, he can purify your motives and teach you wonderful things that you can only learn when suffering humbles you and forces you to pay attention to the deep work the Holy Spirit is doing inside of you.

I'm not suggesting God hurts us on purpose just to watch us squirm in agony. On the contrary; God doesn't hurt us. The world we live in does. Things are breaking down here on earth. People hurt each other. Greed and violence and war and deception are everywhere, and you can't get away from the constant cycle of sickness, poverty, and death. God doesn't create these things to hurt you. He is the very One who wants to rescue broken people from these evil forces. And how does God do that? What is his plan to redeem humanity from the curse?

If your suffering won't go away, it might as well go to work.

It begins with Jesus. God sent his own Son to this earth to live a sinless life and die a horrible death in our place, so that we would not have to be punished for our sin and rebellion.

It continues, however, with us. The plan God began with Jesus was handed off to God's people, Christians, to carry on. Jesus himself promised that we would do even greater works than he did, simply meaning that billions of Christians can accomplish unimaginable good in this world for the glory of God when we understand that God wants to use us in his plan. "Very truly I tell you, whoever believes in me will do the works I have been doing, and they will do even greater things than these, because I am going to the Father" (John 14:12).

And how does he use us, exactly? One way is through our suffering. Consider these words written by Peter, the disciple who spent years with Jesus only to deny him at his crucifixion, and then was restored to lead the New Testament church:

> But if you suffer for doing good and you endure it, this is commendable before God. To this you were called, because Christ suffered for you, leaving you an example, that you should follow in his steps. (1 Pet. 2:20–21)

Does this mean it is God's will for me as a Christian to suffer? At first glance, the answer seems simply . . . yes. But let's consider a more nuanced reading of these verses.

This Scripture states that it is God's will not that you simply suffer aimlessly, randomly, or mindlessly but that you suffer for the purpose of doing good and, more importantly, that you endure that suffering. Therefore, God does not orchestrate purposeless suffering in your life but rather, on the contrary, redeems your suffering, giving you the grace to endure it for the purpose of serving as a witness to the power of the gospel. People—our children, our spouse, our friends, our boss, our extended family, even skeptical non-believers—will observe the way we handle suffering, and they'll learn from us. When they see us endure the same kind of hurts and hardships they experience while remaining humble, faithful, and prayerful before God, they'll pay close attention, curious about the source of our strength.

When it comes to suffering, sometimes the way we overcome is to simply, humbly, and faithfully endure.

To put it another way: there is always a bigger story encompassing the painful place in which we find ourselves. God is

92

always up to something much bigger. And while we may not focus on or even be aware of the bigger God-story in the midst of our suffering, the God-story is still there.

When it comes to suffering, sometimes the way we overcome is to simply, humbly, and faithfully endure.

Nothing testifies to the deep, authentic reality of God's presence in the life of a believer like watching that believer keep their eyes on Jesus while enduring hell on earth. Observing a Christian cry out to God in confusion, pain, and anger, while maintaining the faith to keep calling, to keep weeping, to keep reaching out in hope and trust, is perhaps the greatest apologetic for the Christian faith the world will ever see. Watching Wilkes Skinner suffer through one tragedy after another while keeping a steadfast faith was the very thing that drew me to Jesus as a boy. I couldn't turn away, fascinated by my pastor's unwavering strength in the face of events that should have crushed him. Our suffering has the power to change those who are watching us suffer.

Our suffering has the power to change those who are watching us suffer.

Our Pain Has the Power to Transform Us

Suffering also has the redemptive power to change the person who is enduring it. Author Shannon Evans speaks to this very aspect of suffering and how God uses it as a tool to transform us into more patient, tender, understanding people. She writes:

> My husband and I adopted an 11-month-old boy with a traumatic past. We assumed love would be enough, that the power of God would come, that he would be healed of it all in time.

93

Instead, he suffered. In fact, he seemed to suffer more as the years went by. . . . We prayed and believed in all the ways we knew how, but nothing brought about change or comfort. God, it seemed, was silent. Could we trust a God who wouldn't heal, at least not in the way we expected Him to?[1]

Their pain and confusion brought the Evans family to a place of vulnerability with God where they asked deep, existential questions about his character and whether or not they actually believed he cared about them and their little boy. Yet in their doubt, they continued to cry out to God. This was not an abandonment of their faith. On the contrary, they pressed in harder and deeper, putting their full weight on the God they followed. Evans writes:

We began to taste the implications of Jesus becoming human, of Him binding Himself to us and to our poverty. We experienced greater love for mankind than we had ever known, more compassion than we could ever muster up in the past. We let ourselves be ripped open, and we made the choice to sit still.

I once doubted a God who wouldn't set a little boy free. Now I recognize that He used that suffering to transform the boy's parents into the ones he needed: ones who, rather than will away his messy places, could sit down and link arms with him and say "me too."[2]

Evans and her husband eventually realized God's plan was counterintuitive to their own ideas of how things should turn out.

Maybe God isn't interested in changing the situation you're in right now. Maybe his agenda is to change you, and he's using a tough situation to do it. How else can we grow in humility? What other way is there for us to learn patience? What better means to make us more compassionate and understanding of the suffering of others than for us to know deep suffering, and to experience the sustaining grace of God?

The way we face trials, tests, and pain is with hope; we look back at the grace God gave us before, and we trust him to do the same again. We prepare our minds to endure another hard season, faithfully believing that grace will be there for the next battle. This is exactly what Peter wrote about two thousand years ago, and it's still true today:

> So prepare your minds for action and exercise self-control. Put all your hope in the gracious salvation that will come to you when Jesus Christ is revealed to the world. (1 Pet. 1:13 NLT)

Christ is revealed not only in the second coming we await but also right now—every time we hurt, every time we receive bad news, every time we're afraid, every time our world comes crashing down on us. Jesus is there, with us, in these very moments of pain, suffering, and fear. He comes to us with grace and love and walks through the valley of the shadow of death with us. You may not get an exemption from suffering but you'll get a companion. And isn't a companion better than an exemption, especially when

Maybe God isn't interested in changing the situation you're in right now. Maybe his agenda is to change you, and he's using a tough situation to do it.

that companion is Jesus himself? Drawing close to Christ in seasons of suffering has the power to change us in ways that coasting through a pain-free life never could.

Nothing has the power to transform us from proud, self-sufficient people into humble, tender saints like suffering. It cuts deep, down into the place where the Spirit dwells and operates and cuts out the cancers of pride and selfishness, replacing them with grace and understanding. Choose to embrace the place God has you, even if it is a place of suffering. Stop asking *Why me?* and start asking *What are you trying to change in me?*

Reject the lie that good people don't suffer. They do, every single day. The truth is, when we suffer, God can do something redemptive through it, even when we can't see it or understand it. Because at the very least, suffering strips us of all pretense and forces us to face this truth: we don't know that God is all we need until God is all we have. That's what I learned watching my pastor endure his season of suffering. He relied on God's strength and provision. He modeled absolute surrender. Later in my own life, I revisited those memories as I experienced this truth firsthand during times of loss and grief. Christ really was sufficient for me when my mom had a stroke and my dad's business floundered, when my aspirations to attend college were challenged, when my parents were dying, and when I was filled with fear that I would be alone.

> *Suffering strips us of all pretense and forces us to face this truth: we don't know that God is all we need until God is all we have.*

As Shannon Evans writes, "Human suffering is inescapable. But we get to choose whether we become consumed with seeing it pass, or whether we are willing to open up and let it change us."[3]

If we can learn that one lesson alone, the suffering we endure is worth it.

Next Steps

Here are a few questions to help you lean into the pain you may have experienced in the past or the struggle you're currently facing. Consider how God can leverage this suffering or these challenges for a greater purpose in your life (or for the sake of someone close to you).

1. What is the most painful thing that has ever happened to you?

....

....

....

....

2. Have you ever asked yourself what lesson God could teach you or how he could humble you and change you through that painful experience?

....

....

....

....

3. Have you had a Wilkes Skinner in your life, someone who has reflected God's strength in a time of weakness?

....

....

....

....

4. What if God wants to use you as a Wilkes Skinner for someone else? Would you be willing to be used by God in that way? Who might God be asking you to mentor right now?

....

....

....

....

5. What hard thing are you enduring right now that God could leverage in order to make you more like Jesus? How are you responding to that situation?

....

....

....

....

5

love and intimacy

Understanding God's Design
for Human Sexuality

THE LIE: "Sex is no big deal."

THE TRUTH: A sexual relationship *is* a big deal, and it needs a spiritual covenant and an emotional commitment to survive and thrive.

> Flee from sexual immorality. All other sins a person commits are outside the body, but whoever sins sexually, sins against their own body.
>
> 1 Corinthians 6:18

> Each person actually changes the very structure of the brain with the choices he or she makes and the behavior he or she is involved in.
>
> Joe McIlhaney, MD, and Freda McKissic Bush, MD[1]

A young lady raised her hand from the middle of the humid gymnasium. I called on her from my place on the stage, and she stood up to ask her question. "Who do you think you are?" she accused, anger and defensiveness lacing her words. "You come in here and try to scare all of us with your stories and statistics. But you don't know what you're talking about. Sex is no big deal. I've had sex with lots of guys and even a few girls, and I'm fine! I love it and I'm gonna keep on doing it 'cause it's fun. And what do you know, anyway? You said you're a virgin! You don't know (expletive)."

In more than twenty years of speaking to school assemblies all across America, my exchange with that feisty young woman still stands out as one of the most memorable. I was used to talking about difficult and uncomfortable topics with teenagers. My message focused on the importance of making wise decisions based on the outcomes of personal choices. I warned students about the dangers of drug abuse, underage drinking, and sex before marriage. I would use humor and personal stories to draw them in, and then get serious, changing my tone when I related my own story of being born to a fifteen-year-old mother who gave me up for adoption or about attending the funerals of my classmates who had lost their lives because they thought they were bulletproof to the consequences of stupid decisions.

I was even used to the unscripted, unpredictable nature of the question-and-answer sessions that followed my talks. But that day I was stunned by the young woman's declarations. This teenage girl had so embraced the lifestyle of partying and sex that she was willing to stand up and admit to more than one thousand of her friends and peers that she'd had numerous sex partners, with no concern for how she might be seen or what people might say about her. That was a first for me. I didn't want to embarrass her any further than she had already embarrassed herself, so I had to think quickly.

After the student body calmed down, I simply responded with a challenge. "I know you think that sex is no big deal today, but one day you will change your mind because reality eventually catches up to us all," I told her. "So I'll make a deal with you. You live your way and I'll live mine. You sleep with whoever and I will wait until I'm married. And if we ever meet up again in the future, let's see who regrets it. Deal?" You could hear a pin drop. She yelled at me dismissively from the bleachers, "Yeah, whatever. I'll never see you again if I'm lucky."

Fast-forward twenty years. I was about to preach in a small church not far from the high school where that awkward exchange had taken place all those years ago. A woman approached and sat beside me on the front pew as people milled around the small sanctuary. She smiled knowingly, looking half-shy and half-scared.

"You probably don't remember me," she said, "but I just wanted to tell you that you were right. I do regret it." It was her, the girl from the gym who stood up and proclaimed in front of the whole school that, "Sex is no big deal!"

"You predicted this day would come," she added. She went on to confess that the patterns and habits that had once seemed fun had eventually led her to severe depression, drug abuse, divorce, and a suicide attempt. "Everything you said that day to us was true. Now I'm living for Jesus and I'm back in church, but I wish I had listened," she admitted. "I wasted so many years, years I can't get back."

I never actually thought I'd see her again. But reality had, after all, caught up with her. Just as it eventually catches up with each of us.

101

The Fear of Missing Out

What's the big deal with having sex if it's not hurting anyone?

Who cares who I have sex with? It's my body and I can do what I want with it.

Sex is just physical, so why do people get so worked up over it?

If sex is a private matter that only affects the people who are doing it, then it's nobody else's business if the people having sex are consenting adults, right?

Each of these statements is a lie.

I have no desire to police anyone's personal decisions. It's true that you can do whatever you wish, so long as you don't break the law. I am not challenging your individual liberty to make personal choices; rather, I am warning you that those choices have consequences. Questions like those listed above reflect the deep brokenness of sinful hearts, hearts that need the love and grace of Jesus. These questions uncover a self-centered view of sex, not the kind of sacrificial love Jesus modeled for us. A heart that is not redeemed by Christ will want pleasure, power, and material objects for its own sake, not for the sake of others.

> *The lie we hear and the lie we tell ourselves is that sex is no big deal. The fear that fuels this lie is the fear of missing out.*

The lie we hear and the lie we tell ourselves is that sex is no big deal. The fear that fuels this lie is the fear of missing out. We are afraid we won't be able to experience love, intimacy, or feeling desired without sex. We want to feel loved and to feel pleasure; we want to feel secure and desired; and we believe we are able to walk away from sex unaffected any time we want to.

102

This is both spiritually and physiologically impossible. You can't have sex with your body and not have sex with your soul. If you think sex is no big deal, you are believing a lie. Let's look at the truth about the effect of sex on our bodies, minds, and souls.

What Sex Is the Best Sex?

People are entitled to their own opinions and can make their own decisions, but the research tells us that the best sex happens in the most stable relationships. Scientific evidence supports a view of sex that aligns with a traditional Christian perspective: abstinence before marriage, faithfulness within marriage, and grace and forgiveness in Christ for sex outside of marriage. Scientific research can help us make better decisions about our lives and the future selves we want to become.

Joe McIlhaney, MD, and Freda McKissic Bush, MD, of the Medical Institute for Sexual Health spent years studying the physical effects of sexual activity on the human brain and body, and they released their conclusive findings in the fascinating book *Hooked: New Science on How Casual Sex Is Affecting Our Children*. While our culture preaches "sex is no big deal," the scientific evidence proves otherwise.

For example, according to McIlhaney and Bush,

> It appears that the most up-to-date research suggests that most humans are "designed" to be sexually monogamous with one mate for life. This information also shows that the further individuals deviate from this behavior, the more problems they encounter, be they STDs, non-marital pregnancy, or emotional problems, including damaged ability to develop healthy connectedness with others, including future spouses.[2]

What better way to be "sexually monogamous with one mate for life" than in a committed marriage relationship? McIlhaney and Bush add,

> The riskiest sexual situations by far are those that involve an increasing number of sexual partners with no commitment whatsoever. The younger teenagers are when they initiate sexual activity, the more sexual partners they will be likely to have by the time they are interviewed again in their twenties. Sexual behavior for this young group, once it has commenced, *appears almost compulsive*. This certainly correlates with neuroscientific findings that sex has an addictive effect on the brain.[3]

According to the facts, lots of sex with lots of people, or any sex without the serious commitment of a monogamous relationship, are very risky sexual situations and often lead to problems connecting to others and "compulsive" sexual habits. But doesn't this contradict the prevalent cultural attitude about sex? Anyone who talks about abstinence is dismissed as a religious nutcase or a Puritan. Those who hold to a Christian view of sexuality are labeled as closed-minded and old-fashioned. This includes me. This used to hurt my feelings and make me feel insecure. Now I just don't care anymore. Not only have I seen the real-life effects of believing lies about sex but there is a mountain of scientific data and research that supports what we all know is true: sex is a very real and powerful force, and it should be treated with great care and caution.

The truth is, sex is a big deal.

A sexual connection needs a spiritual covenant and an emotional commitment or it becomes a total catastrophe. Like a house needs a solid foundation to stand on, physical intimacy alone cannot sustain a relationship. It will eventually implode under its own weight. It is covenant, commitment, and grace that hold up the weight of two people, together, for a lifetime.

Sex is more than an animalistic appetite that expresses itself as a biological urge. It's a profound spiritual union of two physical bodies and two spiritual souls. The biological and the spiritual work together when two human bodies and souls unite in sexual intimacy. To say or assume this is no big deal is to misunderstand the essence of what it means to connect with another human being. Don't be overcome by the cultural forces that feed you lies about love and sex.

> *A sexual connection needs a spiritual covenant and an emotional commitment or it becomes a total catastrophe.*

The way out of the lie that sex is no big deal is to replace it with truth—to recognize the scientific facts alongside the biblical instruction that can better inform us and the spiritual healing that can restore us.

Brains, Bonds, and Chemicals

Let's start with the scientific facts. As we all intuitively know, there's a lot more going on inside the human body during physical intimacy than just getting butterflies in your stomach or experiencing an increased heart rate. Thousands upon thousands of chemical reactions take place when two people experience attraction and sexual intimacy.

You've probably heard about adrenaline, serotonin, estrogen, and testosterone. These chemicals, and many more, are actively involved in our sexuality. But experts can now explain how and why sex affects us so radically. Doctors and scientists have used new medical and technological advances and noninvasive brain scanning to see what happens to human bodies when they have sex, and even more importantly, when they have sex without boundaries. The findings are as fascinating as they are frightening.

Somewhere in a digital warehouse, Google, Apple, Facebook, and the like are storing my emails, messages, playlists, photos—basically all my digital information. When it's stored in "the cloud," this information never goes away. This is how your brain stores experiences, events, and memories—all the data and information from your entire life—especially when they are physical and sexual in nature.

Neurons, the primary cells in the brain, communicate through connections called synapses. A synapse is like an electronic signal, something like an email or a text message. There are more than one hundred trillion synaptic connections in the brain (more than all the internet connections in the world combined), and each one of them communicates, sends, and stores all your feelings, desires, fears, wants, dislikes, thoughts, and memories.

Dopamine is a messenger chemical that produces a good, rewarding feeling when a person does something exciting. It floods the brain during sex, causing the synapses to send and receive signals. Dopamine locks the memory of the exciting event in the brain and creates a desire to repeat that activity so that we can experience the same stimulating sensation again. This involuntary chemical reaction happens in the pre-frontal cortex of the brain, the same area that's used to make important, complex decisions. The problem, however, is that the pre-frontal cortex is not fully developed until we are in our mid-twenties, which means a teenager lacks the ability to make wise decisions in light of the consequences of those actions.

Meanwhile, the more sex we have, the more dopamine is released, and the more addicted to the feeling we become. We naturally crave more. It's quite literally a drug. Simply put, the dopamine released in the brain during sex makes us feel the need and desire for more sex.[4]

In addition to dopamine, women also release a chemical called *oxytocin* during romantic physical contact and sexual intercourse. Oxytocin is a "bonding" chemical that helps women build trust when they get close or intimate with a man, and it's released regardless of her sexual partner's intent. Whether she is engaged in a one-night stand or a committed marriage, oxytocin ensures a woman will experience an overpowering desire to bond with a man after sex. This is the woman's chemical cement, and it works great if she's married to the guy she sleeps with. If she's not, it's like ripping her heart out of a cement cast. This is especially dangerous for an adolescent girl in a sexual relationship, who, as Drs. McIlhaney and Bush point out, "may therefore find herself, because of the normal effect of her brain hormones, desiring more physical contact and trusting a male who may be using manipulative pledges of love and care only to get her to have sex."[5]

The male equivalent of oxytocin is called *vasopressin*, a chemical that causes married men to bond with their wives but does actual physical damage to the male brain when sex takes place casually outside of a monogamous relationship. It's been nicknamed the "monogamy molecule" because it causes the man to feel attachment to a woman during physical intimacy, in much the same way oxytocin works in females.[6]

For both females and males, the more sex is had without the stability of love and trust in marriage, the more destructive the habit becomes. In fact, pornography, oral sex, experimentation, and casual sex actually damage the brain and its ability to function properly, especially in men. "They do not realize that this pattern of having sex with one woman and then breaking up and then having sex with another woman limits them to experience only one form of brain activity common to humans involved sexually—the dopamine rush of sex," explain McIlhaney and Bush. "They risk damaging a vital, innate ability to develop the long-term emotional attachment that results from sex with the same person over and over."[7] Or, to state it another way: "The pattern of changing sex partners therefore seems to damage the ability to bond in a committed relationship. The inability to bond after multiple liaisons is almost like tape that loses its stickiness after being applied and removed multiple times."[8]

While our culture normalizes sex without boundaries, science is proving that when we believe the big lie that sex is no big deal, we set ourselves up for disappointment and pain.

While our culture normalizes sex without boundaries, science is proving that when we believe the big lie that sex is no big deal, we set ourselves up for disappointment and pain. Wanting sex for the pleasure without the responsibility is like wanting the taste and pleasure of food without the calories. When a person approaches food this way, it can lead to bulimia, a painful and destructive illness in which a person consumes whatever food is desired and then purges it from the body by vomiting. Approaching sex this way leads to a kind of emotional bulimia, in which you crave the rush of an orgasm or the security of love, fulfill the desire with sex or a "hook up," and then feel the emptiness of loneliness and disconnection once the rush has diminished.

The bottom line here is that you can't trick your body. Science wins out, which is exactly the way God designed it to work. The truth always wins out over a lie.

The Disastrous Consequences of Destructive Sexual Habits

We can't outsmart God. If we break his laws and abuse the bodies he gave us, we suffer. Our bodies are more than cells and atoms. They are intelligent and sensitive and must be treated with care because they are all we have. We can't live anywhere else but in our own bodies, and we must live in our own bodies for the duration of our life on earth. When we misuse our bodies in sexual relationships with other people (who also have bodies like ours), the effects will linger and remain in our bodies.

Scientific research and evidence prove that destructive sexual habits have disastrous consequences for years to follow. Remember our discussion of dopamine earlier in this chapter? As I mentioned, the release of dopamine in pleasurable activities, such as sex, triggers the body's desire for more of what caused the pleasure. This cycle can lead to addiction (it's why the more chocolate and caffeine we ingest, the more we crave it, and it's also why drug addicts crave another hit), especially when the pre-frontal cortex of the brain is not fully developed.

The bottom line: the earlier you start having sex, the more addicted you become to it. This wouldn't be so bad if it were something as simple as playing basketball with your friends or watching your favorite show on TV. But sex involves bodies, and those bodies have brains and feelings. What we do with our bodies matters. There are consequences, both physically and emotionally. Consider these statistics:

- 20 percent of girls using birth control pills get pregnant within six months of having sex.
- 1 out of 5 teen couples using condoms get pregnant within a year.
- Half of all teen girls using any kind of contraception get pregnant within a year of having sex.
- 80 percent of unmarried teenage fathers never marry the mother of their baby.
- 80 percent of unmarried teenage moms eventually go on welfare to survive.
- 70 percent of unmarried moms never receive any financial support of any kind from the fathers of their babies.[9]

Consider also that today in America, more than seventy million people have a sexually transmitted disease (that's about 1 in 5 people), and that every year there are approximately nineteen million new cases. Of those new cases contracted every year, half of them are in people under the age of twenty-five.[10]

Unfortunately, consequences go beyond even teen pregnancy and STDs. Take the rampant problem of divorce, for instance. "Numerous studies show that when people have had sex before marriage, they are more likely to divorce when they do marry later on," explain researchers J. R. Kahn and K. A. London.[11] And it gets worse. Researchers conclude:

> Divorce is not the sole measure of the health of one's attachment or connecting ability. Perhaps as important is the finding that individuals who have had sex before marriage are less likely to experience marital happiness. They are more likely to have difficulty adjusting to marriage and less likely to experience happiness, satisfaction, and love.[12]

Or, to state it more positively: "Now, with the aid of modern neuroscience and a wealth of research, it is evident that humans are the healthiest and happiest when they engage in sex only with the one who is their mate for a lifetime."[13]

Think about the implications of this for a minute. Our minds and bodies crave sex and romance because of the promise of the pleasure it will bring us. But that's only part of a bigger story. The whole truth is that people who have sex outside of a marriage covenant find it more difficult to be happy in a relationship and are more likely to fail once they do get married. In other words, the pursuit of momentary pleasure can lead to a lifelong struggle with unhappiness.

The Good News

The good news is that our biology works in our favor when we engage in sexual intimacy as God designed. As McIlhaney and Bush explain:

> When two people join physically, powerful neurohormones are released because of the sexual experience, making an impression on the synapses in their brains and hardwiring their bond. When they stay together for life, their bonding matures. This is a major factor that keeps them together, providing desire for intercourse, resulting in offspring, and assuring those offspring of a nurturing two-parent home in which to grow.[14]

In other words, the strong desire for sex originates in the brain, and sexual activity floods the brain and the body with hormones and chemicals that lock in the memories of the strong emotions associated with that experience. The longer two people stay together, the better they are bonded. Just as scientists have

111

proven that sex is addictive and destructive outside of monogamy, they have also proven that within marriage, both the spouses and their children have the greatest chance to experience love, stability, and happiness. Marriage is a healthy place for those memories and images. Anything outside of monogamy has the potential for emotional harm.

I'm not a member of a vast conspiracy to keep Americans from enjoying sex. I'm simply pointing out the truth, because if you really want to understand the complex power of sex and have a better chance of enjoying it for a lifetime (and not just a handful of scattered experiences), following God's design is the best way. Regardless of how mainstream and acceptable sex without boundaries becomes in any culture, the facts are unfazed by the trends and the lie evaporates when the truth is revealed.

There's a reason for this. God designed sex to flourish within its proper boundaries—in other words, within a trusting marriage in which both parties have promised their lives to each other. Outside of those healthy boundaries, sex is destructive. Think of sex like fire. When it is contained in its right place it can bring warmth and comfort. When it escapes its proper environment, it can do serious damage. The safety of a marriage covenant is the place for sex. Anything outside of that will cause pain and destruction.

Sex outside the context of marriage leaves a path of destruction in its wake: depression, anxiety, divorce, loneliness, regret, unhappiness, disease, unwanted pregnancy, and even poverty. The institution of marriage itself even offers stability and financial security. According to *The Wall Street Journal*, in 2012 the overall percentage of American families consisting of a married couple living at poverty level was just 7.5 percent, compared to 33.9 percent for families headed by a single mother.[15]

Sex itself is not to blame, because sex is a good gift given to us by God for our pleasure and our flourishing. It is when people try to violate the way God made our bodies and our brains by having careless sex outside of the safety of a covenant marriage that we pay a price. God knows what's best for us. He designed our bodies. He understands how they function and how they should be used and protected. He's provided instruction through his Word. He's given us common sense and the science that supports what he has told us in Scripture. God has made provision for us. It begins by understanding his intent and design for sexuality. This is how you overcome the lies swirling around this issue.

God's Provision

So what if you've already messed up? Is it too late? Are you doomed to a life of shame and regret?

Absolutely not.

First, we've all messed up. Unless your first name is Jesus and your last name is Christ, you're a long way from perfect (and so am I). It's never too late, and you're not damaged goods. Our sexual sins and relationship regrets don't disqualify us from experiencing love and tenderness and the joy of marriage.

Truthfully, we're not pure and holy based on our performance or our perfection but rather a Person. Jesus alone is the source of our purity and holiness, because he is the source of our forgiveness. Just because you mess up doesn't mean you give up.

Remember the cycle we talked about in the introduction? The lie circles around your mistakes, looking for a place to land and plant the roots of shame. It *infiltrates* your thoughts through memories of bad relationships and mistakes you now see, in retrospect, you could have avoided.

Next the lie *insinuates* that you're not only dirty but stupid. It tells you that you should've known better. You should've listened to your parents or your pastor. You thought you would be the exception to the rule, but you were wrong, and now you feel like you wear a scarlet letter everywhere you go.

Then the lie *intimidates* you by convincing you that your past failures translate to future isolation and loneliness. No one will ever want to love you or marry you once they find out all that you've done.

Finally the lie *re-creates* your identity by attacking your self-worth, convincing you that it's impossible to ever enjoy intimacy or sex with your spouse because it's too late; you messed up too badly and even God can't fix things now.

God, however, has made a provision for you (and for every one of us). It's called repentance. We're not destined for a life of loneliness and shame because we've looked at porn, or cheated on our spouse, or had a one-night stand in college. When we're humble enough to ask God to forgive us, he will. Every single time. "If we confess our sins, he is faithful and just and will forgive us our sins and purify us from all unrighteousness" (1 John 1:9).

We overcome the lie by believing what God has told us and living according to his truth. God loves his children, and he would never give us boundaries unless they were for our own benefit and blessing. He knows that suffering follows careless sex. He hasn't left us on our own to try to figure it out. God instructs us to respect the institution of marriage and to be careful that our sexuality is rightly understood. As Paul wrote to the Hebrews: "Marriage must be respected by all, and the marriage bed kept undefiled, because God will judge immoral people and adulterers" (Heb. 13:4 HCSB).

This verse is as straightforward as it gets. Marriage is the God-ordained institution within which sex should be celebrated. It provides stability, trust, safety, and connection. It should be respected, not tossed aside and ignored. The "marriage bed" is obviously referring to sex within a marriage. The apostle Paul instructs the Hebrews, and us, to keep that marriage bed undefiled (pure, clean), because marriage is the proper context for things that happen "in the marriage bed." On the other hand, when sex is practiced outside of the context of marriage, there is no safety net. To put it bluntly, God takes sex seriously because sex deeply affects his children whom he dearly loves. Remember, we protect what we value. God values us and wants to protect us. You should value yourself by protecting your sexuality and your heart.

We protect what we value. God values us and wants to protect us. You should value yourself by protecting your sexuality and your heart.

Human Bodies

In the beginning of creation, God made us in his own image, meaning that in our bodies we reflect God—his likeness and his glory. The same physical bodies that suffered the effects of the fall will be restored and one day look and be like God originally designed them. As Paul reminded the Philippians: "He will transform the body of our humble condition into the likeness of His glorious body, by the power that enables Him to subject everything to Himself" (Phil. 3:21 HCSB).

God gave us bodies, and everything that happens to us happens in the context of our physical bodies. What we eat and drink affects us. What we breathe, what we see, what we hear, and what we touch affects us. Breathing cigarette smoke causes cancer. Drinking antifreeze will shut down our kidneys. Placing our hand on a hot stove will burn our flesh. Given this, don't you think that sex, which incorporates all of your senses at once, would have a lasting effect on your body? Your body matters, and what happens to your body matters. As the theologian John A. T. Robinson points out, the concept of "body" is a major theme throughout God's story in Scripture:

> It is from the *body* of sin and death that we are delivered; it is through the *body* of Christ on the cross that we are saved; it is into His *body* the Church that we are incorporated; it is by His *body* in the Eucharist that this Community is sustained; it is in our *body* that its new life is to be manifested; it is to a resurrection of this *body* to the likeness of His glorious *body* that we are destined.[16]

Our bodies feel the curse of the fall and need to be saved, so God sent his Son to earth with a real human body to redeem us from that curse, and his real human body was crucified and resurrected. God then promises us that we, too, will have real resurrected bodies one day. Moreover, Scripture tells us that the church is the body of Christ, and that we as members of that body will one day experience the restoration of all things. Author and scholar Lauren Winner says it brilliantly:

> *Bodies* are central to the Christian story. Creation inaugurates *bodies* that are good, but the consequences of the fall are written on our *bodies*—our *bodies* will sweat as we labor in the fields,

116

our *bodies* will hurt as we bear children, and, most centrally, our *bodies* will die.[17]

It's not just our souls that will be redeemed and restored at the resurrection but our bodies as well. We'll have resurrected bodies like Jesus. Our physical bodies will age and die, but they will also be raised and changed so that they can enter into God's fully restored Kingdom. If you've ever doubted the importance of the human body, read what Paul said to the church in Corinth:

So it is with the resurrection of the dead:

> Sown in corruption, raised in incorruption;
> sown in dishonor, raised in glory;
> sown in weakness, raised in power;
> *sown a natural body, raised a spiritual body.*

If there is a natural body, there is also a spiritual body. . . .

> Like the man made of dust,
> so are those who are made of dust;
> like the heavenly man,
> so are those who are heavenly.
> And just as we have borne
> the image of the man made of dust,
> we will also bear
> the image of the heavenly man. (1 Cor. 15:42–44,
>   48–49 HCSB, emphasis added)

The human body that experiences pain, fear, love, and joy will be transformed from a natural body like that of Adam (made of dust) into a spiritual body that will never die and will somehow reflect the glory of its Creator in its original design. This has serious implications for how we treat our bodies and the bodies of other people. As Winner explains, "Bodies are who we are and where we live; they are not just things God created us with, but means of knowing Him and abiding with Him."[18] We cannot experience love or God using any other medium than our bodies.

God's Body

What really blows my mind, however, is exactly *how* God saved us from sin and death. He could have chosen a million different ways to redeem us and restore us from the fall, but the plan he crafted was specific to a particular Human Being with a particular body, a body that would feel physical pain, suffering, and death before it would be resurrected. This all happened so we could have a restored relationship with the God who originally created us in his own image (which in some mysterious way means that God has a body that he revealed fully in his only Son, Jesus Christ, who came to earth as a man). Peter, one of Jesus's closest friends and disciples, explains the importance of Jesus's body in our redemption:

> He Himself bore our sins
> in His body on the tree,
> so that, having died to sins,
> we might live for righteousness;
> you have been healed by His wounds. (1 Pet. 2:24
>   HCSB)

Therefore, since Christ suffered in the flesh, equip yourselves also with the same resolve—because the one who suffered in the flesh has finished with sin—in order to live the remaining time in the flesh, no longer for human desires, but for God's will. (4:1–2 HCSB)

God crowned his creation with human beings, whom he gave bodies. We are God's image-bearers. God chose to reveal himself to humanity in a human body. God planned to redeem us from the fall with a human body. God will one day restore us completely with new, glorified spiritual bodies. So let's think about our bodies a little more carefully.

Because Jesus's body overcame the grave, our bodies are redeemed from sin and are now the temple he lives in, and will one day overcome death.

Our bodies reflect God's image, were fashioned after his likeness, and are the sole means by which we live and bring glory to God. Through his broken, crucified body, the curse of sin is removed and we have the promise of resurrection and new life. Because Jesus's body overcame the grave, our bodies are redeemed from sin and are now the temple he lives in, and will one day overcome death:

> Run from sexual immorality! "Every sin a person can commit is outside the body." On the contrary, the person who is sexually immoral sins against his own body. Don't you know that *your body is a sanctuary of the Holy Spirit* who is in you, whom you have from God? You are not your own, for you were bought at a price. Therefore *glorify God in your body*. (1 Cor. 6:18–20 HCSB, emphasis added)

God doesn't just want to save your soul. He wants to save your body, because your soul belongs with your body. They go together. What you do with your body affects your soul, so remember that his salvation for you is for every part of your body, for eternity. "If the fall is written on the body, salvation happens in the body too," Winner explains. "The kingdom of God is transmitted through Jesus' body and is sustained in Christ's

Body, the church. Through the bodily suffering of Christ on the cross and the bodily resurrection of Christ from the dead, we are saved."[19]

When we understand the beauty of the human body and the intricacy with which God designed us, we can walk in the truth of his glory revealed in us and not fall for the lies that destroy God's temple. As image-bearers who reflect the glory and majesty of the living God, we have a higher calling than we often realize.

Science supports what God has been saying to us since creation. We must reorient our convictions based on the revelation of God's story of redemption, accomplished through the crucified and resurrected body of Jesus. Our human bodies reflect the gospel, and we are blessed to enjoy all good things with our bodies, including love, intimacy, and sex. When we understand this, we can overcome the lies we've listened to and the shame we've lived with for the mistakes we've made.

As one older lady once told a group of us in college, "If God ever created anything better than sex, he must have kept it for himself!" I fully agree. Sex isn't God and it isn't gross. It's a good gift from a good God and can (and should) be enjoyed for his glory and our good.

Next Steps

As you think about your own personal perspective on sexuality and intimacy, here are a few questions to move you deeper into understanding some of the ways you process your past relationships, expectations for intimacy, and personal desires for sex.

1. When you hear the word *sex*, what is the first thought, word, or idea that comes to mind?

   ....

   ....

   ....

   ....

2. Did you grow up in a home where your parents avoided all conversations about sex, or were they open to teaching you about it and having healthy conversations about it as you grew older? How might this have impacted your understanding of human sexuality?

   ....

   ....

   ....

   ....

3. Is there a sexual experience from your past that you're still hung up on emotionally? Is there something you can't quite get over or forget?

   ....

   ....

   ....

   ....

4. How much sexuality are you willing to tolerate in your entertainment (TV shows, movies, music, social media)?

   ....

   ....

   ....

   ....

5. Do you have a close friend you can confide in regarding your sexual struggles, battle with lust, or past regrets?

....

....

....

....

6. Do you and your spouse talk honestly about your expectations, desires, and feelings that revolve around your sexual intimacy?

....

....

....

....

6

fighting temptation
with faith

And Knowing Your Victory Is in Christ

THE LIE: "I can't resist temptation."

THE TRUTH: Temptation to sin *can* be thwarted, and it begins with your submission to and reliance on the power of the Holy Spirit in you.

Do not be overcome by evil, but OVERCOME evil with good.

Romans 12:21

Watching "The Marshmallow Experiment" YouTube videos was like tasting chocolate for the first time. I couldn't get enough. Again and again I watched the kids on my computer screen dive to the depths of human desire, forced to fight the greatest temptation of their lives thus far: to refrain from eating a giant marshmallow placed in front of them.

Despite the promise that they would be rewarded with a second marshmallow if they could resist the one set before them for twenty minutes, one after another (with a few exceptions), the children fell prey to the primordial hunger that seems to drive us all to do something, take something, watch something, eat something, or drink something we know we should not. They had no idea they were being filmed. I had no idea something could be so mesmerizing. I found myself laughing hysterically, all the while relating to their inner struggle, as the kids touched, smelled, and licked the marshmallows, trying, largely unsuccessfully, to withstand temptation.

The first marshmallow experiments took place in the 1960s at Bing Nursery School and were conceived by Stanford psychology professor Walter Mischel in an attempt to understand the power and nature of self-control. The children who participated in the original study were followed and studied into their fifties. As teenagers, those who showed the power to delay gratification in the original tests scored higher on their SAT scores. In adulthood, subjects who had initially waited the twenty minutes without eating the marshmallow had a lower Body Mass Index on average. In their fifties, the people who had originally delayed gratification as children had lower rates of obesity. There was a clear correlation between self-control and overall well-being.[1]

The conclusion was twofold. First, some kids seemed to have a natural inclination toward delayed gratification. But second, and perhaps even more important, even those children who had "failed" the original test were able to learn self-control when they were later taught a few simple techniques.

There's something worth noticing here. We as adults can be encouraged and motivated by the fact that even if we are genetically predisposed to certain vices, like the children in the study, we can learn to overcome "the urge" when taught how to wait, say no, and delay gratification. So whether we struggle with the urge to smoke a cigarette or the desire to splurge while shopping, the impulsive cravings we feel can be overridden by the cognitive effort of thinking about the greater reward in the long term versus the quick reward in the short term.[2]

Of course, I realize it can be more complex than this. Addictions and urges, especially of the chemical nature, often require detox, rehab, and retraining the brain. Emotional and psychological health is often only reached through therapy and counseling, along with spiritual practices such as prayer, meditation, and worship. But the point is simply that we can say no. We're not predestined to always give in to temptation. Your destiny is not predetermined.

Raise the Stakes, Change the Context

Whether we succumb to the lure of money, a margarita, or a marshmallow, the power that woos and dominates us is called *temptation*.

Back in the '70s, comedian Flip Wilson became famous by stating repeatedly on television, in response to doing something naughty, "The devil made me do it!" This seems to be how a lot of people think about temptation. It may be easier to blame the devil when I binge on a half-gallon of ice cream or when I lose my patience and yell at my kids, but the fact is, I know which of my choices are unhealthy or wrong. Few of us have ever had a gun held to our head when we clicked on that link or told that lie or snuck in that little verbal jab. We do it all on our own without much coercion.

Have you ever said to yourself, *I just can't resist that temptation*? Yeah, so have I. I get it. I understand how powerless you feel, because I've felt that way too. It's easier to dismiss our failure to resist destructive urges by saying we just can't stop than it is to face the hard truth, which is this: we usually give up too easily when we could have put up a better fight.

> *We usually give up too easily when we could have put up a better fight.*

The lie we tell ourselves is that we simply can't resist temptation. The truth is, we are deceiving ourselves with a grand delusion. We do this all the time.

Take, for example, the temptation of pornography. If you struggle with pornography, you are constantly and incessantly tempted to look at naked people (whether on a smartphone, tablet, magazine, or TV screen). The more you succumb to the temptation, the easier it is to tell yourself that you just can't say no.

But what if someone offered you $100 million in cash to film you twenty-four hours a day, challenging you to go six months without looking at porn? Could you resist the temptation? For that kind of money, I suspect you could. So it's really not impossible, is it? You could overcome the temptation.

Or what if you're tempted to gossip and speak negatively about others? What if you had a device implanted in your head that delivered an electric shock every time you said something negative about someone? Like a puppy being trained to stop short of the underground electric fence at the edge of the yard, you'd learn to resist the temptation to speak ill of others. So it's not really impossible, right?

It could be food. It could be sex. It could be gossip or rage or spending too much money. Regardless of our actual object of temptation, it's a lie when we tell ourselves we cannot resist "the urge." The fact is, we can overcome temptation when the stakes are high enough and the context changes.

Let me give you another example. The temptation to have sex before marriage is really high when you're in bed with your honey in the dark after midnight. But what if you change the context and the stakes? Imagine thinking about having sex outside of marriage when you're sitting in the stands at a college football game among seventy-five thousand screaming fans. The context has changed. You'd never entertain the thought of taking your clothes off and having intercourse. Not only has the context changed but the stakes are too high. Doing something so unthinkable would mean embarrassment, public humiliation, a possible prison sentence, and countless social media memes (with a few late-night jokes from Stephen Colbert and Jimmy Fallon thrown in for good measure).

> *The fact is, we can overcome temptation when the stakes are high enough and the context changes.*

Declaring you are powerless to resist temptation is a lie. When you realize what's at stake and you understand the context, you can walk away from tempting situations, even if you've given in dozens of times before. There is a way out of this lie.

The scenario I just painted about the football stadium was meant to be humorous, but the truth is, the stakes *are* that high. In fact, they're even higher than we might initially realize. According to the Bible, the ultimate conclusion to succumbing to temptation is as bad as it gets. It's death.

When tempted, no one should say, "God is tempting me." For God cannot be tempted by evil, nor does he tempt anyone; but each person is tempted when they are dragged away by their own evil desire and enticed. Then, after desire has conceived, it gives birth to sin; and sin, when it is full-grown, gives birth to death. (James 1:13–15)

Evidently, temptation is the first step down a dark road that leads to bad things . . . like death! So this is, indeed, a big deal. It's impossible to *remove* all temptation from your life, but it's totally possible to *resist* temptation. Resistance is the way out. That's the escape hatch. And resistance is possible because we have a personal relationship with Jesus, which enables us to submit to his authority and lean on him for strength when we're weak. As James advises, "Submit yourselves, then, to God. Resist the devil, and he will flee from you" (4:7).

> *It's impossible to remove all temptation from your life, but it's totally possible to resist temptation.*

This is exactly how Jesus resisted temptation when the actual, literal devil came to him and tried to tempt him to sin (during a forty-day fast without food, by the way). Jesus resisted the temptations thrown at him by going back to the Word of God and saying it out loud. In Luke 4, Satan tempted Jesus three times, and all three times Jesus resisted temptation by remembering Scripture. He quoted from the Old Testament book of Deuteronomy not once, not twice, but three times in a row. This is our example to follow: God's Word is the first step for us to take in order to defeat temptation when it comes knocking.

Our strength is not in human effort. Our strength to fight temptation comes from our willingness to submit to God, humbly relying on him. When we submit to the Lordship of Christ and his power to help us, we can rest in his ability instead of focusing on our inability.

So does this mean we don't do anything beyond remembering a few verses? Is there anything required of us, since Jesus has already made us holy through his sacrifice on the cross?

And if the victory has already been won and sin has been defeated, why does temptation keep assaulting us and oftentimes win?

Many people get frustrated with their failure to resist the temptations they face daily. They believe they have victory in Christ but they feel weak and experience defeat in their daily lives. They try to rely on the strength of the Holy Spirit. They pray and fast, join an accountability group, and read the Bible, but they often keep giving in to the same temptations and get frustrated when they fail. Then they feel guilt and shame. I admit that I've felt the same way. Is there a way forward through these struggles?

A Lesson from History

My grandfather was in the Navy in the South Pacific during World War II. He spoke about the war sparingly, but the stories he did tell captivated me.

In 1941, Europe was being overrun by Hitler's army. Jews were being systematically exterminated, and the United States was bombed by Japan. There seemed to be little hope of winning against such strong enemies. It would take more than soldiers and bullets to turn the tide of the war. If the human race were to remain free, it would require a concerted effort and a superior plan to defeat the Nazis and the Japanese. Effort alone would never be sufficient, and there's a priceless lesson to learn from this important moment in history.

The Allies had to win in three different arenas: ground, air, and intelligence. Germany had a superior army and air force in Europe. Japan had a strong navy and air force in the Pacific. We would have to do more than match their strength. To defeat them, we would have to outwit them.

Allied forces stormed the beaches of Normandy to establish a ground presence for the Army to launch an offensive. Aircraft carriers transported fighters and bombers to Europe to push back the German attack on London and establish air superiority. Meanwhile, naval and ground forces converged in the South Pacific islands as Albert Einstein and other scientists secretly worked on the first atomic bomb in a covert program called the Manhattan Project.

The plan did not depend on just one point of attack. The success of winning the war was predicated on all three elements: the ground, the air, and intelligence. We had to put troops on the ground. We had to get planes in the air. And we had to have better information. We would overcome our enemies if we could establish superiority in these three areas. We did it, and we won the war.

Sin is a serial killer and it will not settle for anything other than total dominion over your life.

Is there something we can learn here, specifically in our fight against temptation? I believe there is.

You will never win this battle simply by trying harder. Temptation is stronger and more experienced than you. Sin is a serial killer and it will not settle for anything other than total dominion over your life.

Let's take a page from the Allies' playbook. Instead of focusing on one aspect of your struggle, employ multiple weapons against temptation. The Allies fought to dominate land, air, and intelligence. I believe we can employ three tactics to gain victory over temptation. But first, we need to understand exactly how we are called to fight.

The Power to Fight

The ability to launch an offensive against the power of sin comes from the power of the Holy Spirit, who dwells in you and makes your heart his home. If you think for a second that you can outsmart sin, it will assassinate you before you can blink. Our ability to wage war against insecurity, shame, and regret is rooted in the power of God that is at work within us right now.

The apostle Paul puts it this way:

> For this reason I kneel before the Father, from whom every family in heaven and on earth derives its name. I pray that *out of his glorious riches he may strengthen you with power through His Spirit* in your inner being, so that Christ may dwell in your hearts through faith. (Eph. 3:14–17, emphasis added)

Our strength is not in a formula or human effort. Our strength is the Holy Spirit. We will win when we submit to the Lordship of Christ and allow him to dwell in our hearts through faith in his power, not our own. Any effort that stands upon our own strength will only frustrate us as we grow more and more fatigued and eventually wallow in our own failure. The real battle is fought when we remember how powerless we are against an enemy as strong and seasoned as sin. If we can remember the strength of the Spirit who is at work in us, renewing us and transforming us, then we're positioned to fight and win.

I have talked to thousands of students and adults over the past thirty years who have been frustrated by their inability to resist daily temptations. In their hearts they believe they have victory in Christ, but they consistently experience defeat in their daily lives. For many, it seems as if they're doing something wrong. They try to rely on the strength of the Holy Spirit. They read verses like the ones quoted above from Ephesians 3. But instead of experiencing victory, they just keep giving in to the same urges. Often this results in feelings of guilt and weakness. Some of them begin to question their salvation. They wonder if they are even true Christians.

The following is an excerpt from a message a young woman sent me on Facebook. She gave me permission to share this with you, and I think it symbolizes the internal struggle every Christian feels when he or she can't get total victory over sexual sin.

Dear Clayton,

I know you are a busy guy, traveling and preaching all the time. But I really need your help because I feel like I am always trying so hard to get victory in the area of sexual purity, but I just keep failing over and over again. I don't know who to turn to. I listened to all of your messages on relationships and you kept talking about finding our strength in Christ. You said that Jesus had defeated sin in me when he died on the cross and was raised from the dead. I am a Christian and I have been saved for almost ten years, but I don't know HOW to win against sexual temptation. You said I had victory in Jesus, but if I really do, how does that work when I am being tempted to mess around with my boyfriend? I am not a virgin. I really love my boyfriend and we're both Christians. We know it's wrong to sleep together, but we just can't stop. We pray and we've even read the Bible together, but nothing works. I'd love to know HOW we can stop messing around because when you were preaching about it, it sounded so true and so easy. But then my boyfriend and I were together just hours after we both heard you preach, and we messed up again! I am so frustrated! I don't even know if I am a Christian anymore. I am doubting my own salvation. I am so confused. If I were really saved, I feel like this wouldn't be so hard. HELP!

Have you ever felt like her? I know I have. I also know it's not easy to break free from patterns of temptation, sin, and shame. But in Christ, it is possible. Just like the Allies had to win the war on three fronts (air, land, intelligence), we can wage war in three very effective ways to win against the discouragement and frustration that always come along with falling into temptation.

It's not a sin to be tempted, because even Jesus was tempted to sin. You can learn how to overcome temptation and stop it dead in its tracks before it builds momentum and overwhelms you.

The Battle Plan

The great British pastor and evangelist C. H. Spurgeon once said that even though sinful thoughts may rise, they must not reign. Our goal should be to stop sinful urges before they take control. Just because they rise in you, they don't have the right to reign over you. It's not a sin to be tempted, because even Jesus was tempted to sin. You can learn how to overcome temptation and stop it dead in its tracks before it builds momentum and overwhelms you. This plan of attack stands on the victory of

Christ over sin while simultaneously moving forward based on your decision to fight against the ongoing power of temptation. It's easy to remember because it's catchy. You can memorize the plan by saying the steps aloud several times.

To resist temptation, do these three things:

HATE IT.
STARVE IT.
OUTSMART IT.

1. **Hate it**. A decision must be made. You must take a position of absolute hatred toward sin. Decide you won't tolerate it. Get angry about the way it offends God. Despise the negative ways it hurts you and your body. Stop feeling sorry for yourself and take the offensive. No more whining and complaining! An attitude of complete intolerance is the only attitude that will work in the war against temptation.

2. **Starve it**. French general Napoleon Bonaparte once reportedly said that an army marches on its stomach. In other words, if you want to defeat temptation, quit feeding it. If you're tempted to binge on junk food, avoid Krispy Kreme when the "Hot Now" sign is illuminated. If you're tempted to look at porn, install filters on your tablet or laptop. If you're tempted to compare your "boring life" to the "exciting life" of others, stay off Facebook and Instagram for a season. Be ruthless; starve your appetite for sin. The longer you starve it, the weaker the temptation will become.

3. **Outsmart it**. Get ahead of your enemy by predicting the ways you are tempted *before* you are tempted. Devise a plan that can't fail. Stop vacationing in Vegas every year if you struggle with gambling. Ask a friend to hold you accountable

in your new dating relationship if you're tempted to go too far physically. If you struggle with the urge to check your email first thing every morning, turn off your smartphone every night at nine before you go into your room for bed. If you know the images of sex scenes will stick in your head when you should only be thinking about your spouse, read reviews of movies before you buy a ticket to avoid sexual content. Outsmart the temptation to sin.

A passage in the Old Testament lays the foundation for the "Hate It, Starve It, Outsmart It" approach. I've gone back to these verses so many times I can quote them from memory. Check out these verses from Psalm 119, and notice the words that are emphasized:

> How I love Your instruction!
> It is my meditation all day long.
> Your commands make me *wiser* than my enemies,
> for they are always with me.
> I have more *insight* than all my teachers
> because Your decrees are my meditation.
> I *understand* more than the elders
> because I obey Your precepts.
> I have *kept my feet* from every evil path
> to follow Your word.
> I have not turned from Your judgments,
> for You Yourself have instructed me.
> How sweet Your word is to my taste—
> sweeter than honey to my mouth.
> I gain understanding from Your precepts;
> therefore I *hate* every false way. (Ps. 119:97–104
>   HCSB, emphasis added)

The writer hates it. The last line plainly states that he hates every false way. I know *hate* is a strong word. You may not feel comfortable using it because you were taught that you should never hate anyone. But this is not about hating a person—this is about hating what God hates, and God hates sin! Get over your fear of the word *hate* and realize that hating sin is the first step toward defeating it. God hates sin. You belong to God. You must hate sin too.

The writer starves it. He says that he's kept his feet from every evil path to follow God's Word. He decided he will not feed any evil desire; he will not walk in the path that leads to wicked places. Instead of moving toward sin and temptation, he moves away from them by pursuing something better: the Word of God. Read God's Word, meditate on his wisdom, and build your relationship with Christ through prayer, worship, and service. Your faith will strengthen as you feed it; temptation will weaken as you starve it.

> *If we trust God, we will do what he says. And if we want to know what he says, we find it in his Word.*

The writer outsmarts it. The writer says that God's commands make him "wiser" than his enemies, His decrees offer him more "insight" than his teachers, and he "understands" more than the elders because he obeys God's precepts. And where can you find God's commands, decrees, and precepts? In his Word. You don't have to devise a complex plan full of intricate details and tricks to gain victory over temptation. The way you outsmart sin is to read the Bible, know the Bible, and obey the Bible. Jesus is Lord and he calls the shots. If we trust God, we will do what he says. And if we want to know what he says, we find it in his Word.

Outsmart sin by applying the ancient wisdom of Scripture. It's tried, tested, and true.

Adapt Your Battle Plan according to Your Enemy

First you need to *adopt* the "Hate It, Starve It, Outsmart It" battle plan, and then you need to *adapt* it to your particular temptations. Though we all struggle with temptation, those desires will look different in each of our individual lives. You may be tempted toward same-sex attraction, compulsive spending, or chronic lying. You might be tempted to manipulate others to get what you want. Loneliness or depression might tempt you to return to a former boyfriend or girlfriend.

Whatever your particular temptation, prepare yourself to get creative and flexible. Adapt your strategy according to your enemy. Your enemy is sin. Jesus has given you victory over sin. You are learning to live out that victory by waging war against temptation daily. You are learning to rely on the power of the Holy Spirit to resist those temptations by getting aggressive and taking the offensive against sin by hating it, starving it, and outsmarting it.

Let's look at how this plays out in real life. One of my best friends, Steve (not his real name), had a strange but effective way of adapting this approach to his own personal temptation.

He and his wife had only been married a short time. Because she had shopped at Victoria's Secret, their address was added to the store's customer database, and as a result they began to receive Victoria's Secret catalogs at their home. Now, if you know anything about Victoria's Secret, you know there really aren't any secrets. It's pretty much all out in the open. The pictures in the sales catalogs may seem harmless to many women, but for most guys, a Victoria's Secret catalog is one step short of soft-core porn. The images of shapely female supermodels in their underwear become locked in a man's mind, which can lead to a curiosity and appetite for even more titillating images. Just as marijuana can become a doorway drug for other addictions, Victoria's Secret catalogs can become a doorway for men (and even some women) to crave more graphic images.

Steve wanted to cut off the temptation (i.e., starve it) before it arrived because he hated the idea of fantasizing about any woman besides his wife. He called Victoria's Secret and asked to be removed from their mailing list, but the catalogs kept coming. He called again, but they kept appearing in his mailbox. He tried to outsmart that temptation by throwing the catalogs away, but even the thought of them in the trashcan was tempting, and he imagined retrieving the catalogs from the garbage.

So he adapted his strategy to address his particular situation. When a catalog arrived, he took it into his bathroom, lifted the toilet seat, and plunged it into the toilet. He swirled the catalog around several times to ensure it was good and soggy, and then he dropped the waterlogged magazine into the trashcan. Steve was determined to cut off all possibility of being drawn back to the temptation he'd already resisted. The dirty toilet water deterred him from digging the tempting catalog out of the garbage.

Steve hated it, starved it, and outsmarted it, and when outsmarting the temptation failed the first time, he adapted his strategy. He got serious. He cut off the food supply by starving his mind of the potential to look at those pictures. He adapted his battle plan to the nature of the temptation, and it worked.

This is war, friends, and if you're going to win the battle against temptation and sin, you will have to adjust your approach to the situation you face. Start with "Hate It, Starve It, Outsmart It," and then tailor your plan of attack from there.

When he goes on the road to preach, another old friend of mine, who is an evangelist like me, practices the same ritual every time he enters his hotel room. To outsmart the temptation to watch pornography, he unplugs the TV, covers it with a towel, and places pictures of his wife and kids in front of it. That's ruthless! He makes it hard to sin and very unlikely that he will give in to that temptation.

You could call this example good old-fashioned self-control, but the key to self-control is that our human effort is rooted in the power of the Holy Spirit. Because he lives in us, we have the power to change our attitudes, habits, and desires. It will take effort to hate it, starve it, and outsmart it, but as the apostle Peter tells us, that effort pays off:

> For this very reason, *make every effort* to supplement your faith with goodness, goodness with knowledge, knowledge with *self-control*, self-control with endurance, endurance with godliness, godliness with brotherly affection, and brotherly affection with love. For if these qualities are yours and are increasing, they will keep you from being useless or unfruitful in the knowledge of our Lord Jesus Christ. (2 Pet. 1:5–8 HCSB, emphasis added)

Fighting from Victory, Not for Victory

Nearly 250 years ago, our ancestors were living under the tyranny of the British Empire. They declared their independence from England and launched the Revolutionary War. The Americans won and we became a free people.

You and I have never once fired a shot at a British soldier but every single day we enjoy the freedom our ancestors won, because they fought a war that was for us. They won the victory for us. We have freedom because of their sacrifice.

Jesus allows us to enjoy the benefits of his victory. Because he was faithful, we can be free.

Like our ancestors fought for our freedom long before we were ever born, Jesus bled and died for our freedom thousands of years before we were alive. He faced an opponent that we could have never defeated, but through his sacrifice on the cross, he triumphed over the enemy. Jesus allows us to enjoy the benefits of his victory. Because he was faithful, we can be free.

It is absolutely paramount that every Christian understands one simple truth in the ongoing fight against temptation. We can actually hate it, starve it, and outsmart it *because* the battle has already been fought and the victory has already been won.

We are not fighting *for* victory. We are fighting *from* victory. When Jesus was raised from the dead, he proved once and for all that all power and authority in the universe and beyond belongs to him. No one had ever defeated the enemy of death before, but Jesus did, and he gave us a glimpse into the power of the Kingdom he came to inaugurate.

The power to overcome temptation is the power of Jesus Christ, and Jesus Christ lives in you through the Holy Spirit. He has made you holy, and *holiness is both a position and a pursuit*. Because you are a child of God by faith in Christ, your position in his family is secure. Because he has filled you with his Holy Spirit, you have the power to pursue holiness and resist temptation from your position as a forgiven, redeemed child of the King.

The ability to live a holy life is found when you submit your will and your ways to the Lordship of Christ, and he gives you his holiness.

The fight against temptation is won by faith—when you trust that Jesus has something better for you than the momentary pleasure you will receive by giving in to your urges and desires. The stakes are higher.

We are not fighting for victory. We are fighting from victory.

The Gospels record the last words Jesus uttered before he died on the cross. He said, "It is finished." This did not mean that he was finished. It meant the mission he came to accomplish had been completed. Jesus lived a holy and perfect life for all of us who could never be holy and perfect on our own. He suffered and died in our place when we deserved to be punished for our sins. He destroyed the work of the devil and the power of sin, not with a sword or a spear or thunder and lightning but through humility and submission to his Father. And in the face of temptation, even face-to-face with Satan himself, Jesus never wavered. He remained faithful to his mission.

When he proclaimed, "It is finished," he declared victory over sin, death, hell, damnation, and judgment. He announced the Kingdom of God in all its power and beauty. God had won and Satan had lost. The curse was reversed, and new life was now available to all who believed in him.

Rejoice as you read these words from Paul declaring Christ as the victor and us the recipients of the bounty of his victory:

> When this corruptible is clothed
> with incorruptibility,
> and this mortal is clothed

with immortality,
then the saying that is written will take place:
Death has been swallowed up in victory.
Death, where is your victory?
Death, where is your sting?
Now the sting of death is sin,
and the power of sin is the law.
But thanks be to God, who gives us victory
through our Lord Jesus Christ!

Therefore, my dear brothers, be steadfast, immovable, always excelling in the Lord's work, knowing that your labor in the Lord is not in vain. (1 Cor. 15:54–58 HCSB, emphasis added)

Jesus's power gives you victory over guilt, shame, insecurity, regret, and temptation. The ultimate battle was fought two thousand years ago. The ultimate victory has already been won. The winner has been declared, and it is Jesus. Because you belong to Jesus, you are also one with Jesus. That means you are just as victorious as he is. His victory is our victory. You are holy in your position as God's possession, and you are empowered to overcome every temptation because Jesus overcame sin for you on the cross.

You are holy in your position as God's possession, and you are empowered to overcome every temptation because Jesus overcame sin for you on the cross.

You are not trying to fight this battle alone. You're not attempting to win victory. The victory is already yours. So start acting like the victor. Learn how to live in the victory Jesus won for you. You are not fighting *for* victory. You are fighting *from* victory.

Next Steps

Let's get concrete about putting some of this into practice. The following questions will help you think about the specific situations you face and how you can reject the lie and resist the temptation. There is no right or wrong—just honest and not-so-honest. Let's aim for honesty here!

1. In a regular day at work, at school, or at home, can you name two or three temptations you face frequently?

   ....

   ....

   ....

   ....

2. On a scale of 1 to 10, with 1 being "I don't even put up a fight" and 10 being "I put on a Kevlar vest and turn into a Navy SEAL," how hard do you usually fight against the common temptations you face daily?

   ....

   ....

   ....

   ....

3. How do you feel immediately after you've succumbed to the temptation to sin? How long does that feeling last? How do you handle those emotions?

   ....

   ....

   ....

   ....

4. Of all the various temptations you face daily, what is the one that stands out as potentially the most destructive in your life? Explain why this one is different from the rest.

....

....

....

....

Once you've identified the temptation(s) you're ready to tackle, write down your own "Hate It, Starve It, Outsmart It" game plan with specific examples of how you'll resist when the time comes.

7

the pursuit of happiness

Finding Safety, Security,
and Satisfaction Not in Worldly Things
but in God

THE LIE: "Money will solve all my problems."

THE TRUTH: Money masquerades as our savior, offering counterfeit hope to hungry souls. Only our real Savior offers us the true identity, security, and happiness we yearn for.

> Whoever loves money never has enough; whoever loves wealth is never satisfied with their income.
>
> Ecclesiastes 5:10

Born and raised in the backcountry of West Virginia, Jack Whittaker had a tough start to life.[1] Through hard work and self-discipline, he eventually launched a successful construction company, and by the time he was in his mid-fifties, his company employed a staff of more than fifty and had made him a millionaire several times over. He lived a quiet life, loved his family, and gave generously to his church.

All that changed on December 24, 2002, when Mr. Whittaker stopped at the C&L Super Serve to pick up two bacon biscuits for breakfast. He also bought a lottery ticket. Christmas night, as he watched TV, he discovered he had missed the record-breaking jackpot by one number. He chalked it up to bad luck and didn't think too much of it. To Jack Whittaker, the lottery was just a fun game. Besides, he'd already made his millions through hard work; he didn't need the money.

Jack Whittaker woke up the next morning to the news that the previous night's broadcaster had read the numbers incorrectly. He looked down at the ticket in his hand and listened as each number matched up.

With $314.9 million, Jack Whittaker was, at the time, the winner of the largest single jackpot payout in history. After taxes, he walked away with more than $113 million in cash, a world-record payout. On December 26, Mr. Whittaker appeared on live television to accept the first portion of the payout from the governor of West Virginia. In the press conference afterward, he promised to rehire twenty-five workers he had laid off, help build local schools, and start a charitable foundation to help the folks of his own state of West Virginia. He was also going to build a church, help support various pastors, and tithe the biblical amount of 10 percent of his winnings. "I just want to thank God for letting me pick the right numbers. Or letting the machine pick the right numbers," he said.

Mr. Whittaker was about to learn a surprising lesson. He wanted to use money to solve problems. He didn't anticipate how many problems that money would cause.

Initially everything seemed fine. He bought the convenience store clerk who had sold him the ticket a new Jeep and a house, and gave her a check for $44,000. He also donated $14 million to the foundation he established. For a few months, he kept his promises. He gave away millions and helped others. His money seemed to solve some problems.

But then the dream began to turn into a nightmare.

It started at the Pink Pony strip club in rural West Virginia. One morning at five o'clock, he called the police to report a large amount of money missing from his Hummer—more than $500,000 in cash. Less than three months later, he crashed the same Hummer into a concrete median. He refused all sobriety tests, and in his report the arresting officer noted he had smelled alcohol on Whittaker's breath. Jack Whittaker's statement to reporters after his arrest was defiant: "It doesn't bother me, because I can tell everyone to kiss off!"

The following year, on a cold January night, he was so intoxicated he parked his car in the middle of the street, only to return a short time later to find the $100,000 in cash he had left on the passenger seat missing. He was charged with drunk driving.

Jack Whittaker's life continued to spiral out of control. He assaulted and threatened to kill a bar owner. He was sued for sexually assaulting a gambling attendant at a racetrack. His wife divorced him. His granddaughter's boyfriend overdosed at the family's house. His granddaughter overdosed and was found dead in the woods. His daughter was found dead. Even the woman who sold him the ticket at the convenience store was stalked and harassed by people who falsely assumed she had received ten percent of the winnings.

Within a few years of cashing in his record-setting lottery ticket, Jack Whittaker estimated he'd been involved in more than four hundred legal actions. In 2009, seven years after winning all those millions of dollars, he sobbed as he told reporters, "Since I won the lottery, I think there is no control for greed. If you think you have something, there's always someone else who wants it. I wish I'd torn that ticket up."[2]

The man who had more money than most of us will ever have was spiritually, relationally, and financially bankrupt. He had suffered a cost no amount of money could recover.

More Money, More Problems?

If only Jack Whittaker could have taken these words to heart:

> Keep your lives free from the love of money and be content with
> what you have, because God has said,
>> "Never will I leave you;
>>> never will I forsake you."
>> So we say with confidence,
>>> "The Lord is my helper; I will not be afraid.
>>> What can mere mortals do to me?" (Heb. 13:5–6)

We mortals are overcome by the lure and the love of money because we get duped by its bogus promises of safety, ease, and pleasure. Maybe the late rapper Notorious B.I.G. was on to something when he recorded the prophetic song, "Mo' Money, Mo' Problems." His own money and the success it brought him was part of what brought his young life to an early end. And he's certainly not the only one.

We believe more money will solve our problems, all the while watching another athlete, another movie star, or another celebrity destroy their life in spite of (and sometimes because of) their riches. Think about Whitney Houston, Elvis Presley, Robert Downey Jr., Zac Efron, Amy Winehouse, Billy Joel, Demi Moore, Eminem, Charlie Sheen, Evander Holyfield, and Kurt Cobain. Their wealth fueled their vices and their addictions, at least in part. Some bounced back. Others didn't.

We mortals are overcome by the lure and the love of money because we get duped by its bogus promises of safety, ease, and pleasure.

As Mrs. Doubtfire, Mork from Ork, and dozens of other characters, Robin Williams brought millions of people laughter and joy, but on the inside he wrestled with alcoholism, drug addiction, and depression, and was filled with a hopeless despair money could not cure. "Cocaine is God's way of telling you you are making too much money," he once said.[3] Robin Williams realized money, and the addictions and vices it fueled, was not the answer to any of the problems he faced. He took his own life in 2014 at his home in California.

Consider as well the people who either declared bankruptcy or lost everything they had despite their wealth: Pamela Anderson, Lindsay Lohan, Hulk Hogan, Willie Nelson, MC Hammer, and Mike Tyson, who earned over $400 million in his boxing career but was penniless after his career ended.

The Guinness Book of World Records once named the "King of Pop," Michael Jackson, the world's most successful entertainer, but in 2007 he declared bankruptcy, unable to repay the $25 million loan on his Neverland Ranch. Despite the fact that he had sold more than 750 million albums and made more than

$500 million during his career, he was $500 million in debt when he died.[4]

These are celebrity examples—people most of us have heard of but have never met. But the fact is, the number of people we do know—family members, friends, coworkers—who have found themselves struggling with money is staggering. None of us is immune to the kind of mess money can create.

For example, money and finances are the leading cause of stress and anxiety in marriage as well as for singles:

> Money and stress do seem to go hand in hand for many Americans, whether they're in relationships or not. A study released by the American Psychological Association found almost three-quarters of Americans are experiencing financial stress at least some of the time, and nearly a quarter of us are feeling extreme financial stress.[5]

And yet, despite the stress money causes, we still crave more of it, even at the expense of our health. In a 2011 study conducted by Cornell University, many Americans said they would prefer more money over eight hours of sleep. Specifically, they would choose a higher-paying job that only allowed them six hours of sleep over a lower-paying job where they could get seven and a half hours of sleep. So whether it be greed or financial necessity, money and the things it can give a person often make it preferable to a full night's rest for many of our friends and neighbors. This alone indicates what a big deal money is and has always been.[6]

Counterfeit Hope to Seeking Souls

During college, my two best friends and I drove to the Grand Canyon on a whim and decided, since we were so close to "Sin

City," that we would visit Las Vegas. I didn't gamble but I wanted to see the inside of a casino. We went to the MGM Grand and, unbelievably, we ran into the basketball star Dennis Rodman. He was surrounded by an entourage of people, including two gargantuan security guards and several scantily clad female "escorts." He was wearing a Rolex watch, had diamond and gold rings on almost every finger, and was betting thousands of dollars on each hand at the poker table.

I politely approached him and asked him a few questions. I remember thinking he seemed royally bored, and he offered only short, generic answers until I asked him, "Dennis, are you happy?"

He stopped playing poker, took off his sunglasses, and looked directly at me. "No, I'm not happy," he stated matter-of-factly. "I haven't been happy since I was a kid. Why do you think I do all this? I'm chasing happiness, but I don't know if I'll ever be happy again. I'm just a lonely millionaire athlete."

Twenty years later, Dennis Rodman still seems to be searching. After he made tearful appearances on *Oprah* and *Celebrity Rehab* with Dr. Drew, court documents revealed that he was too broke to pay child support to his third wife, to whom he owed over $800,000. Despite making almost $29 million in the NBA and winning five NBA championships and playing with the great Michael Jordan, he's now completely broke.[7]

I think of his words often. *No, I'm not happy . . . why do you think I do all this?*

I look around at our nation and our civilization and wonder if our reckless behavior is somehow rooted in our endless and instinctive pursuit of happiness, security, and even identity. But what if having more money isn't the answer after all? What if there is a better way to find the security and identity we crave deep in our souls?

Maybe you've said to yourself, "If only I could pay off the house/credit cards/student loans," or, "Life would be so much easier if I made an extra $20,000 a year." Maybe you believe that changing a few numbers and adding a couple zeroes to the balance in your bank account would radically improve your life and happiness.

Or perhaps, as you read Jack Whittaker's story, your mind leapt ahead to the things that could and would be different if you won $100 million in the lottery—all the people you would help; all the places you'd go; all the good you'd do. I get it. I've thought the same thing.

It's true, at least in part. Money can allow us to do good things. But money won't solve all our problems. Money is no savior. As a matter of fact, it's foolish to think there's a financial solution to a spiritual problem. The root of this lie is the fear of living our life without the things that would make us happy and give us stability. We believe money can buy the life we've always wanted: a life filled with loving family, caring friends, abundance of joy, good health, regular vacations, dependable vehicles, and a nice home. A life free of the fear that one financial setback will throw us into a vortex of anxiety. But is there also a deeper fear at work here?

> *The root of this lie is the fear of living our life without the things that would make us happy and give us stability.*

I believe there is. It's the fear that God can't be fully trusted to take care of us. It's the fear that he may forget about us or miss some of our needs. Our lack of trust in God's provision manifests itself as greed, stinginess, work-a-holism, and hoarding. When we subconsciously fear that God won't provide for our financial needs, we act as if we can take care of things without God's help at all.

To be clear, good things and certain possessions can make life more enjoyable . . . to an extent. Good health, a new car, stable relationships, and financial margin are worthy pursuits that God can grant to his children as blessings. I don't want to imply that nice things are incompatible with following Jesus. I personally want to live a debt-free life. My family enjoys a swimming pool in our backyard. Occasionally I even spend the extra money to take my wife on an overnight getaway to a nice resort. But I do not live for these things. As a matter of fact, I lived most of my life without these things.

> *Money can never give you what God alone can provide.*

* * * * * * *

You fall victim to the lie that enough money will fix everything. This lie *infiltrates* your mind when you see other people who have money and you assume they are happier than you are. Next, the lie *insinuates* that if you worked harder, if you were more industrious, if you stopped tithing and giving and kept it all for yourself, you would be happy like all those other people with money. Then the lie *intimidates* you by showing you frightening scenarios of what your life would be like without the safety and security of money. Finally the lie *re-creates* your world, turning you into a greedy, anxious curmudgeon who worries about money and security all the time and never stops to enjoy friends or food or vacations or intimacy or a sunset because you're so consumed with watching the financial bottom line.

What a depressing way to live.

The lie we believe is that money (and the pleasure and security we think it can bring us) is the one thing we need most of all in this life.

But it's not.

In fact, the truth is the exact opposite: money can never give you what God alone can provide. As Paul reminds the Philippians (and us), "My God will supply all your needs according to His riches in glory in Christ Jesus" (Phil. 4:19 HCSB).

We need God. We need his provision, his grace, his love, and his forgiveness. We need his promise that he will sustain us and never leave us and his promise that Jesus is preparing a place for us in eternity, where we will live forever in relationship with God and our sisters and brothers. We need each other. We need the church. We need the Scriptures to guide, convict, and encourage us. Money can't provide these things. Money masquerades as a savior, but in reality it's an impostor, offering counterfeit hope to hungry souls.

Consider the fact that most of the winners of large lottery jackpots end up in worse shape than if they had never won the money in the first place. Large lottery winners face a greater probability of kidnapping, drug overdose, homicide, and bankruptcy—yes, bankruptcy. In fact, nearly 70 percent of those who suddenly receive a large sum of money will lose it all within a few years.[8]

> *Money masquerades as a savior, but in reality it's an impostor, offering counterfeit hope to hungry souls.*

Your biggest enemy when it comes to money isn't your job, family, friends, or coworkers. It's you. No one wants to admit they lack self-control in their spending habits, so the answer becomes, "If I just had more money . . ." This rationale positions you as the victim instead of the irresponsible spender.

So instead of being brutally honest with ourselves about the real issue (overspending, selfishness, no budget, living beyond our means, laziness), we more easily believe the lie that more money could fix everything that's wrong in our lives.

One of the men who worked in my father's motor shop used to joke, "They say money can't buy happiness, but I'd love to try and prove whoever said that wrong!" It is easier to believe money will solve all our problems than it is to get to work at solving our actual problems. The dream of having more money offers the promise of a shortcut. We don't really want the money itself; we crave the false sense of safety, security, and satisfaction we believe money will bring us. But instead, money has a unique way of complicating things.

> *We don't really want the money itself; we crave the false sense of safety, security, and satisfaction we believe money will bring us.*

Follow the trail of the pursuit of money and you will soon stumble into the wake of destruction left by those who went ahead of you. The love of money will overwhelm you and overcome you before you can blink.

The Root of All Evil

The word *evil* is a strong one. It brings certain things and people to mind. Hitler. Racism. Ebola. Terrorism. And for me, spiders and cilantro. But we have to be careful not to lump money into the "evil" category, because just like money in and of itself cannot solve all our problems, money in and of itself is not evil. It's simply a means of exchange, a medium by which we determine the value of things we need or want. Yet it does seem to have a strange, hypnotic effect on the human heart.

The Bible says the *love* of money is the root of evil. Do you see the subtle difference? It's actually our sinful hearts that make an idol out of money. Money doesn't become sinful until we begin to love it and the way it makes us feel when we have it.

In his first letter to Timothy, Paul writes about wisdom for leadership, life, and godliness for himself and the church. He talks about the dangers of false teachers, particularly false teachers who seek selfish gain:

> Those who want to get rich fall into temptation and a trap and into many foolish and harmful desires that plunge people into ruin and destruction. For the love of money is a root of all kinds of evil. Some people, eager for money, have wandered from the faith and pierced themselves with many griefs. (1 Tim. 6:9–10)

These verses pointedly explain how the love of money becomes an insatiable craving that causes pain, harm, ruin, and destruction. These verses are also among the most frequently misquoted. Paul chooses and uses his words carefully, explaining that "the love of money," rather than money itself, is evil. To state it plainly: as soon as you start to pursue the idol of wealth, you start down the path toward destruction. Wealth is not sinful—the driving desire to be rich is. Do you see how radioactive the desire for money can become in the human heart and why it's so essential that you overcome this lie?

As soon as you start to pursue the idol of wealth, you start down the path toward destruction. Wealth is not sinful—the driving desire to be rich is.

I conducted a little experiment while I was writing this chapter. I was interested in fleshing out this idea that "the love of money is the root of all kinds of evil," to see if I could uncover a sinful scenario that couldn't be traced back to a love of money. It was impossible. Every sinful situation I considered, somewhere, somehow had the love of money woven into it. Here are just a handful of examples:

- A young girl is kidnapped from her village in Thailand and sold as a sex slave to a pimp in Bangkok, where she's forced to be a prostitute for years.
- A sixteen-year-old high school sophomore tries pot for the first time, gets high, and eventually moves on to pills, crack, and meth.
- A city is told by officials their water supply is safe to drink, but after the cover-up is discovered, they see that they were lied to and the water was making them all sick.
- Corporate executives continue to rake in millions in bonuses and salary perks while hiding their company's debt and putting employees and investors at risk of losing everything.
- A wife catches her husband looking at porn late one night in his office and finds out he's hidden the addiction for years. It all started when he clicked on a link as a teenager on his computer, a link that led to a website to lure in young viewers to an industry that makes billions of dollars a year.

Do not fear money. Fear falling in love with it.

The scenarios are infinite. Eventually, every problem and every sin and every evil scenario, from world wars to corporate crime, involves the love of money somewhere along the way. So I caution you: do not fear money. Fear falling in love with it.

Jesus and Money

It's no coincidence that many of Jesus's parables, as well as the conversations he had with people in the Gospels, deal with money. Money is mentioned more times in the New Testament than heaven and hell combined. There are over two thousand verses in the Bible dealing with money and possessions. Clearly God wants us to manage our money well and to put it to good use.

Perhaps one reason so many of us struggle with not having enough money is that we don't manage what little bit of money we have well. If we can't handle a little bit, we certainly can't be trusted with a lot.

In Luke 16, Jesus tells a parable about a rich man and his servant who learns a lesson about how to manage money. Then Jesus says, "Whoever can be trusted with very little can also be trusted with much. . . . So if you have not been trustworthy in handling worldly wealth, who will trust you with true riches?" (Luke 16:10–11).

Jesus said this in front of the Pharisees, a group of religious professionals who loved money and the prestige and honor it brought them. To ensure they didn't miss what he was saying, Jesus drove the point home clearly: "'No one can serve two masters. Either you will hate the one and love the other, or you will be devoted to the one and despise the other. You cannot serve both God and money.' The Pharisees, who loved money, heard all this and were sneering at Jesus" (vv. 13–14).

One of the most disappointing conversations Jesus ever had with someone is found in Matthew 19, and it's a poignant indicator of how dangerous lies about money and wealth can be.

> Just then a man came up to Jesus and asked, "Teacher, what good thing must I do to get eternal life?"

"Why do you ask me about what is good?" Jesus replied. "There is only One who is good. If you want to enter life, keep the commandments."

"Which ones?" he inquired.

Jesus replied, "'You shall not murder, you shall not commit adultery, you shall not steal, you shall not give false testimony, honor your father and mother,' and 'love your neighbor as yourself.'"

"All these I have kept," the young man said. "What do I still lack?"

Jesus answered, "If you want to be perfect, go, sell your possessions and give to the poor, and you will have treasure in heaven. Then come, follow me."

When the young man heard this, he went away sad, because he had great wealth. (Matt. 19:16–22)

As far as he's concerned, this man thinks he's a good guy. He's kept the law and played by the rules. He's young, in the prime of his life. He has "great wealth" and resources that should silence all his fears about the future. He wants to live forever, and he thinks maybe Jesus has the answer.

So I have to ask: If his wealth had solved all his problems, why was the man longing for eternal life, and why did he come to Jesus to ask how he could get it? He knew intuitively that there was a deep need in his soul for peace with God and the hope of something lasting and eternal. His wealth had no power to fill that void. Money couldn't buy his soul a place to live for eternity and it couldn't suppress that little voice in his heart that whispered, *There's something more.* In short, the man only seemed to have it all, but deep in his heart he realized he didn't have anything.

This has to go down as one of the most depressing passages in the Bible, because it doesn't say the man doubted Jesus, or called him a liar, or even that he thought Jesus was crazy. He didn't reject Jesus as a person but he sure did reject what Jesus said. The text specifically says the man walked away from Jesus with sadness in his heart. Why? Because he was rich. He loved his money and the life it afforded him. He wasn't willing to give that up. Even for eternal life.

How sad indeed.

In another parable Jesus tells a story of a man who thinks he should tear down his barns because they are too small to hold the bumper crop his fields have just produced, and build bigger barns in their place. His flippant and selfish attitude motivates God to call him a "fool" and even indicate that the man's life will end that very night. It wasn't wrong for the man to have big barns or a successful harvest, but his heart was revealed when he decided to hoard what he had instead of sharing it with those in need around him.

"This is how it will be with whoever stores up things for themselves but is not rich toward God," Jesus says to the crowd at the conclusion of the parable (Luke 12:21). What does "rich toward God" mean? It means that God is better than wealth, that he alone is the treasure that can satisfy us. When our hearts are completely focused on God, we realize he is the ultimate wealth of all things. Being "rich toward God" means counting God greater than all of the riches the world has to offer. All of the world's promises of security and prosperity are like Monopoly money when compared to God's promises of security in his Son, Jesus. Worldly inheritance is insignificant in the light of Kingdom inheritance. The Christian's life does not consist of an abundance of material things but an abundance of faith in a God who can grant eternal life.

Plan Your Work, Work Your Plan

"The plans of the diligent lead to profit as surely as haste leads to poverty" (Prov. 21:5). Once you've identified the lie and found the fear that fuels the lies about money, you're in the perfect place to craft a plan to control your money without it controlling you. If you don't have a plan and stay passive with your money, it will take on a life of its own and begin to control you either with excessive greed or incessant worry and anxiety at how quickly it disappears. As you plan your work and work your plan in regards to the money God will allow you to manage and steward during your lifetime, here are some suggestions for overcoming the temptation to place your hope in something as fickle as finances.

> *Giving is not about God getting the money out of your pocket. It's about God getting the greed out of your heart.*

Be Generous

The overarching command from the Bible concerning money is to avoid being enslaved by the love of wealth and to be generous with your resources. Of the many passages that direct us to give freely to God and others, this one is perhaps the most straightforward:

> Command those who are rich in this present world not to be arrogant nor to put their hope in wealth, which is so uncertain, but to put their hope in God, who richly provides us with everything for our enjoyment. Command them to do good, to be rich in good deeds, and to be generous and willing to share. In this way they will lay up treasure for themselves as a firm foundation

for the coming age, so that they may take hold of the life that is truly life. (1 Tim. 6:17–19)

Generosity is the vaccine for the disease of greed. It forces greed to let go of its death grip on our souls. Tithing, giving, volunteering, and supporting missionaries and non-profit ministries help us exercise the spiritual muscle of generosity, making it stronger as greed grows weaker. Giving is not about God getting the money out of your pocket. It's about God getting the greed out of your heart.

Record Where and How You Spend Your Money

It's essential to get a firm grasp on our money, and the best way to do that is to see exactly where every dollar is going once it leaves our hands. It amazes me how many people have no idea how much money they spend on a monthly basis. We should know, right off the top of our head, how much money we make, how much we spend, and what we spend it on . . . every single month. We can't chart a course toward financial health if we don't know our current condition.

> Be sure you know the condition of your flocks,
>   give careful attention to your herds;
> for riches do not endure forever,
>   and a crown is not secure for all generations (Prov.
>   27:23–24)

Write everything down so you can see it, with an income column on one side and a spending column on the other. Once you understand how much you make and how much you spend, you can create a budget. This allows you to define your limits and plan ahead for the bills you pay on a regular basis, as well as for unexpected emergencies, whether it's a blown car engine or a house roof that needs to be replaced right before Christmas.

Recording exactly where and how you spend your money also lets you see where you waste money on things that could easily be eliminated from your life. Identify these "waste items" and redirect the saved money to an emergency fund (ideally, six months of living expenses). This step is essential, because it teaches you discipline in your finances and frees you to liberate not just your money but your mind from worrying about money all the time.

Here are some questions to guide you as you begin to put together a monthly budget:

1. What is your total income for the year (before taxes) and what is your monthly income?
2. What is your total annual income after taxes? This is the amount of money that you actually take home, and the total amount that you must live on.
3. What are your monthly bills? This includes your mortgage, car payments, student loans, personal loans, credit card debt, power and water bills, health coverage, groceries, entertainment, cable, internet, cell phone, and extra spending.
4. How much do you tithe and give to your church and to ministries you believe in?
5. What payments have you automated?

Pay Down Debt

In addition to tracking your income and expenses, write down all your outstanding debt. The beauty of writing down your debt on a piece of paper is that you can actually see it. Most of us are shocked when we discover how much we're paying every month in interest on debt. This should motivate us to become debt-free as soon as possible, because, as Proverbs 22:7 says, "The rich rule over the poor, and the borrower is slave to the lender." Pick your smallest debt amount and work at paying it off first, then move to the next smallest amount. Paying debt down from smallest to largest gives you a sense of confidence as you build momentum toward living a debt-free life, and a debt-free life frees you to be even more generous with your income.

Start Saving

When I was in my twenties, my former pastor gave me this formula as a simple way to begin to think about money: tithe 10 percent, save 10 percent, and live off the rest.

Simplistic? Sure, but it's a good place to start. Saving is the best way to create financial margin and stability. No one really gets rich quick, and those who do often lose it because they didn't work for it. Saving is actually fun, because it removes much of the anxiety of wondering how we will live in the future.

In Ecclesiastes 11:2, Solomon advises us to "divide your investments among many places, for you do not know what risks might lie ahead" (NLT). This is commonly called diversification, and it simply means not putting all your eggs in one basket. Start with your emergency fund (enough cash to live off of for six months), and once you have that established, take advantage of a Roth IRA. Even if you can't max it out every year, start one as soon as you can and have a monthly amount automatically withheld from your paycheck and deposited directly into your Roth. Simple IRAs are also a good idea, as well as maximizing any matching funds that your employer offers you with an IRA or a 401(k).

Please don't skip life insurance, especially if you are married with a family. There are numerous ways to invest here, from whole life to term insurance, and a good financial coach or a trusted older friend or family member can help you decide which is best for you. Then you can move on to mutual funds, stocks, real estate, and even government bonds.

Proverbs 21:20 says, "the wise store up choice food and olive oil, but fools gulp theirs down." Handling our money wisely allows us to use money as a vehicle to help others, to bless the poor, and to fund the mission of the gospel. Do we really think we would remember the Good Samaritan if he'd only had good intentions? No. He had money, and money was necessary to help the man in need. He was able not only to rescue the man left for dead in the ditch but also to provide him with a place to stay and someone to care for him. He had enough margin that he even paid in advance.

> *Do we really think we would remember the Good Samaritan if he'd only had good intentions? No. He had money, and money was necessary to help the man in need.*

Overall, changing our financial habits can be stressful and sometimes difficult, but it is well worth it. Bringing our money management into line with biblical standards is a responsibility Christians often take too lightly. In this age of financial irresponsibility, being a responsible steward of the money God has given us is a way to be a shining example to a world where instant gratification is more important than future security.

The Proper Place

It turns out money can't solve all our problems after all. Jesus drove this point home with this important question: "What good will it be for someone to gain the whole world, yet forfeit their soul?" (Matt. 16:26). Our real problems are always internal before they are external. Jesus wants us to focus on the human soul, which is of ultimate value.

When we put money in its proper place, it won't become an idol in our life. Money is important, but our eternal soul is of eternal importance. So we *use money* and *love people*. Make sure not to get that backward, because it's easy to listen to the lies about wealth, identity, and success, and if we're not careful, we can begin to *love money* and *use people*. That never ends well for anyone.

Jesus also made us a promise. Knowing all the things we would need in this life, he encouraged his followers to "Seek first the kingdom of God and His righteousness, and all these things will be provided for you" (Matt. 6:33 HCSB). We can believe that promise. Or, as they say, we can take that to the bank.

Next Steps

Although I offered some concrete strategies for how to manage your money in this chapter, I also want to leave you with a few biblical principles we find in Luke 6:27–38, about generosity and living with the discipline of giving. Giving is about much more than money. God doesn't want us to give to get the money out of our pockets but rather to get the greed out of our hearts.

1. Enemies become friends when we give forgiveness.
2. Strangers become family when we give kindness.

3. Takers become givers when we give possessions.
4. Hoarders become helpers when we give money.
5. Hurters become healers when we give mercy.
6. The more we give, the more God will give us to give away.
7. We can't out-give God, but it sure is fun to try!

Here are a few questions to help you begin to take control of your money before it takes control of you.

1. List three things you spend money on that you could live without (entertainment, eating out, etc.).

   ....

   ....

   ....

   ....

2. List three simple, specific ways you could practice generosity immediately (tithing, supporting a local ministry, etc.).

   ....

   ....

   ....

   ....

3. List three things you own that you don't need and that you could give to someone else as a blessing (spare room at your house, extra vehicle, etc.).

   ....

   ....

   ....

   ....

8

forgive us our trespasses

Receiving God's Forgiveness
So That We May Forgive Others

THE LIE: "I can't forgive (or be forgiven)."

THE TRUTH: You can forgive, because you are forgiven by Jesus Christ.

"They will fight against you but will not OVERCOME you, for I am with you and I will rescue you," declares the LORD.

Jeremiah 1:19

Forgiveness . . . is like a Band-Aid that holds the edges of an open wound together long enough for the wound to heal. Though he cannot heal what happened to his wife, nor whatever is wrong with the man who killed her, he must attend to the wound inside himself.

David Von Drehle[1]

The poignant words above appeared in *Time* magazine months after gruesome and senseless shootings took place on June 17, 2015, at Mother Emanuel African Methodist Episcopal Church in Charleston, South Carolina. They refer to Anthony Thompson, whose wife was brutally murdered in front of him. Anthony chose forgiveness. It seems he had to, if the wound that formed inside his soul was ever going to heal.

On June 17, at a Bible study in Mother Emanuel Church, Dylann Roof pulled out a gun and murdered nine church members as they bowed their heads in prayer. Just minutes earlier, they had accepted him with open arms and given him a place to sit among them in their Bible study. He responded to their kindness by turning the church into a crime scene. Nine families, along with a nation, mourned and questioned. How could one person be filled with so much hate?

The internet exploded with support for the families of the victims as well as outrage toward the killer, a white supremacist who hoped to provoke a race war in the very city where the first shots of the Civil War were fired. Many said he shouldn't be forgiven. Roof was placed in solitary confinement for fear that other inmates would murder him before his day in court arrived.

It was determined that Roof was eligible for the death penalty and that he would soon be on death row. This was no surprise. There was no doubt that he had committed these senseless acts of hate and violence. The evidence against him was unquestionable.

Yet something strange was about to happen as the world watched and listened.

In an unusual bond court appearance Friday for Dylann Roof, the families of the victims of the Charleston church shooting gave moving statements about their loved ones, acknowledging anger and pain but praying for the accused killer's soul and telling him he was forgiven.[2]

When the victims' families had their first occasion to meet the killer in a courtroom, the Bible study that had been so abruptly broken up a few days earlier resumed as some of them taught the world a lesson on forgiveness. With hot tears running down my face, I watched as CNN played clips of the grieving family members speaking to Dylann Roof.

"I forgive you," said Nadine Collier, daughter of one of the victims. "You took something very precious away from me. I will never get to talk to her ever again. I will never be able to hold her again, but I forgive you, and have mercy on your soul. . . . You hurt me. You hurt a lot of people. If God forgives you, I forgive you."[3]

"For me, I'm a work in progress. And I acknowledge that I am very angry," said Bethane Middleton-Brown, sister of one of the victims. "We have no room for hating, so we have to forgive."[4]

I don't mean to imply that it was easy or automatic for these loved ones left behind to forgive the killer. To be sure, some of the family members struggled both internally and externally to say anything or to feel anything but anger after the killings. Those who spoke words of forgiveness did not dismiss what happened. Rather they were, in the words of Anthony Thompson, attending to the wound inside themselves.

A courtroom was transformed into a sanctuary, where the world was able to see something impossible and supernatural take place: forgiveness.

No matter how much someone has wronged you and hurt you, they will control you and you'll continue to suffer as long as you refuse to forgive them. It's long been said that refusing to forgive another person is like drinking poison in hopes that it will kill your enemy when it's only killing you. Of course, we know we should forgive those who wrong us. It's a great concept on paper, and the thought of letting something go is exhilarating—as long as we're reading about it in a book or watching it unfold on a movie screen. But when it gets personal, when it's me who has to forgive an offense that wounded me deeply, it moves into a new level of impossibility. And so we believe the lie that we can never forgive.

No matter how much someone has wronged you and hurt you, they will control you and you'll continue to suffer as long as you refuse to forgive them.

We fear that, in forgiving someone, they won't get the justice they deserve.

In the case of the Charleston killings, the family members did not forget Roof's actions. They didn't excuse his racist hatred. Justice will still be administered, and Roof will still pay for his crimes. But those who loved the victims the deepest and who had lost the most were the very ones who, in front of a nation in shock and mourning, exposed the lie that says we cannot forgive. They proved that we can. That we all can. They proved that there's no excuse to live in bitterness and resentment and that there is no offense we cannot choose to forgive.

You can overcome the lie that you can't forgive.

They were also a living testament of the power of God's grace. The families in Charleston forgave because they had been forgiven. The grace they extended was the same grace they had received. They were living out, in real life with its complexities and difficulties, what Jesus taught in the Sermon on the Mount:

This, then, is how you should pray:
> "Our Father in heaven,
> hallowed be your name,
> your kingdom come,
> your will be done,
>> on earth as it is in heaven.
> Give us today our daily bread.
> *And forgive us our debts,*
>> *as we also have forgiven our debtors.*
> And lead us not into temptation,
>> but deliver us from the evil one."

For if you forgive other people when they sin against you, your heavenly Father will also forgive you. But if you do not forgive others their sins, your Father will not forgive your sins. (Matt. 6:9–15, emphasis added)

The Root of the Lie

We often find it hard to forgive others because we don't believe we can be forgiven ourselves. This is the deep, dark root of the lie. The fear underneath the lie that we can never forgive is the fear that we may not be forgiven for the things we've said and done.

Imagine your life is a house, and in that house is a room: your heart. Inside your heart, in a deep, dark corner of your soul, sits an old, dust-covered foot locker, inside of which not only are the wounds other people have inflicted on you but also the words, deeds, and thoughts you keep hidden because you know they were,

> *The fear underneath the lie that we can never forgive is the fear that we may not be forgiven for the things we've said and done.*

and still are, wrong. You've hidden that rickety old box out of sight, deep in your heart, hoping that if you don't see it, it will go away.

The problem is, you can't ever really escape its pull. It's always there, always within striking distance, just a few steps away. You stack stuff on top of it to keep the lid shut, but you know what's inside, and it scares the life out of you.

Dealing with what's inside the box would enable you to put old hurts behind you and move on. But you're afraid that once you crack open the lid, it will be like opening Pandora's box—there's no telling what kind of frightening emotions and memories will emerge. After all, the foot locker that's remained hidden for so long is more than a crate—it's a crypt. And it contains the remains of your regrets. It's full of your sins.

Intuitively, you know you would be better off if you dealt with what's inside the box. But the lie is always whispering, *Leave it alone. Don't touch it. If this ever got out, you'd never recover. It's better to steer clear of something so volatile. Forget about that old box and get on with your life. Those things are in the past. If you open it up, you're stirring up trouble.*

It *infiltrates* your mind with these words and *insinuates* that you can't handle a face-to-face confrontation with those hurtful things inside the box. It *intimidates* you by bullying you with fears from your past and *re-creates* your current world based on the lie that old hurts and past sins are just too hard to deal with and are better off left alone.

But that's not all the lie tells you. It also says, *How could you have been so stupid? How could you have done such a thing! You should feel ashamed of yourself. You're damaged goods now. Look at all these sins. There's no way you'll ever be able to move past this. If people knew about this, they would be so disappointed in you. You'd better keep this hidden if you want anyone to ever love you. You could never be forgiven for all these sins.*

And that is the fear that fuels the lie.

We often allow this lie to control us. Despite the fact that we've been determined to keep our past sins hidden from ourselves and others, deep down, we know the sins we've committed—the hurtful words, selfish actions, and sinister thoughts. We've tried to keep these regrets and mistakes locked away, but they seep out through the cracks and crevices of that old, dilapidated box. Memories of past indiscretions play over and over in our minds, like a song on repeat. Our mistakes get caught in a mental loop, and no matter how many times we replay it, it always turns out the same way. We feel ashamed. We feel condemned. And we stay stuck.

But what if there is a way out? What if there is a way to break the cycle of shame and self-condemnation, to become unstuck?

What if we could overcome unforgiveness?

Give and Take

Thompson put it this way, speaking quietly: "I would just like him to know that—I forgive him, and my family forgives him. But we would like him to take this opportunity to repent. Repent," he repeated. "Confess. Give your life to the one who matters most, Christ, so that he can change him. And change your ways, so no matter what happens to you, you'll be ok."[5]

Anthony Thompson faced the man who murdered his wife and offered him forgiveness. But he also offered him something else: grace—a grace that demanded something of his wife's killer. If Dylann Roof was to know the peace and liberation of forgiveness, he would first have to confess his deeds and repent of his horrible sins, not only to the people he hurt but to God. "Repent," Thompson urged. "Confess. Give your life to the one who matters most."

No matter how much forgiveness was extended to him, it would remain untaken until Dylann Roof owned up to his sin. To get the gift, he would have to give something up. He would have to admit his wrongs. No excuses. No explanations. It's been said that the only thing required of us to receive grace is to be humble enough to admit that we need it.

Consider the parable of the unforgiving debtor Jesus tells Peter in Matthew 18. In the story, a master canceled a large debt owed to him by one of his servants after the servant begged for forgiveness. Almost immediately after his own debt was forgiven, however, the servant then turned around and refused to forgive a much smaller debt owed to him by a fellow servant. "'Pay back what you owe me!' he demanded. His fellow servant fell to his knees and begged him, 'Be patient with me, and I will pay it back.' But he refused. Instead, he went off and had the man thrown into prison until he could pay the debt" (Matt. 18:28–30). When the master heard about his servant's unwillingness to forgive another's debt, he called the servant in. "'You wicked servant,' he said. 'I canceled all that debt of yours because you begged me to. Shouldn't you have had mercy on your fellow servant just as I had on you?'" (vv. 32–33).

God doesn't grant forgiveness because we are good. He grants forgiveness because he is good.

To break the power of the lie that you can never forgive or be forgiven, you must come broken and empty-handed to God with only one thing in your possession: humility. Forgiveness may be offered but it is not truly received until you humble yourself before God and recognize your own culpability and guilt. Humility is the missing element in this parable. The servant may have begged for forgiveness but clearly he didn't truly own his sins; he didn't truly repent. He didn't come humbly before his master. He received forgiveness, but because he didn't accept ownership of his sins with humility and true repentance, he wasn't able to reap the full benefit of forgiveness, which is the ability to then forgive others.

Understanding that we have sinned and been forgiven by the Father allows us to extend grace to others. God gives forgiveness. We take forgiveness. Only then are we able to forgive.

This is the way out. This is how we overcome. We open up the dusty old box full of radioactive material. We expose its shameful contents to the light. We break the cycle of shame, insecurity, and fear. We find forgiveness, not only for the things we've done but for the harm done to us by others. We can forgive. But we have to give something before we can get something.

> *Mercy is granted when we do not get what we deserve. Grace is granted when we get what we don't deserve.*

This give-and-take only happens when we stop running from our shame, when we cease all attempts at justifying or dismissing our deeds, and when we fall on our knees in humility before God. We acknowledge that all our sins are against him first, before they are against anyone else. God gives forgiveness. We take it. Grace is a gift that we didn't earn and we don't deserve. God doesn't grant forgiveness because we are good. He grants forgiveness because he is good.

To truly understand the miracle of forgiveness, we have to look at it from God's perspective. As the maker of the universe, all things are truly his. Therefore, every transgression against another person (the sins we've committed and the ones committed against us by others) is against God primarily and against our neighbor secondarily. When we focus only on the horizontal nature of the sin, we miss the vertical reality that God's law has been broken and his holiness offended.

God is both our judge and defense attorney. As our judge, he has the authority to punish or pardon sin. As our defense attorney, he stands by our side and defends us against accusations of worthlessness, shame, and insecurity. What's more, Jesus has already served our sentence. You and I were guilty of sin, deserving punishment and banishment, but Jesus stepped up and stood in our place. He received what we deserved. He endured what justice demanded. Jesus paid our debt when he died on the cross in our place.

Jesus offers both mercy and grace. Mercy is granted when we do not get what we deserve. Grace is granted when we get what we don't deserve. In other words, God grants mercy when he withholds punishment from us; he grants grace when he pardons and forgives us.

If you haven't accepted God's forgiveness of your own sins, you will continue to believe the lie that it's impossible to forgive those who have sinned against you.

Forgiveness does not happen without faith. In order to be free from the lie that you can't forgive or be forgiven, you have to believe that God has made it possible for you to be forgiven and that he has also given you the ability to extend that same grace to others. To put it another way: you can't give what you don't have. If you haven't accepted God's forgiveness of your own sins, you will continue to believe the lie that it's impossible to forgive those who have sinned against you.

This is the way out: believe that you are forgiven in Jesus. Open the box of sins you have hidden away and refused to acknowledge. Repent of your sins, receive the free gift in humility, and then, by the power of the Holy Spirit, you can begin to move toward forgiving others. Once we see ourselves as the recipients of undeserved forgiveness, it doesn't seem so impossible to extend forgiveness to those from whom we have withheld it. Your forgiveness of others will only go as far as your surrender to Christ.

Freedom Is Superior to Slavery

Forgiveness is not just for the offender. It's for the offended as well. It's not about setting the offender free from consequences and justice. It's about setting you free from the bondage of bitterness.

The truth is, we often struggle to forgive because we feel like we are owed a debt by the person who wounded us. Perhaps that person stole something from us when they lied to us, or took our money, or physically harmed us, or snubbed us, or damaged our trust with their unfaithfulness. We want the offender to pay us back, to settle the account, to make things right. We want the debt squared away. Perhaps we subconsciously even enjoy holding that debt over their head in our hearts.

> *It's not about setting the offender free from consequences and justice. It's about setting you free from the bondage of bitterness.*

But what if the debt is never repaid? What if the offender doesn't understand the depth of the hurt we experienced? Or, as in the case of Dylann Roof, what if the offender took something as precious as a human life, a debt that could never, ever be repaid?

179

The fact is, the debt may never be repaid. The person who wounded you may never repent, apologize, or attempt to make amends. As long as you wait on the guilty party to make recompense for their sin against you, you will die a slow, internal death. Resentment will settle like a plague in your heart. You'll spend years, even decades, replaying the past over and over again, each time growing more angry and anxious.

I know, because I've been there.

Back when I was a young minister, twenty-two years old and fresh out of college, a friend approached me in great distress. He was in trouble and needed some help. "Clayton, I know you have such a good heart. I've seen you help people before, in a lot of different ways," he said. "And I'm hoping you love me enough to help me like you've helped other people you barely even know." My friend then asked if I would loan him $2,000.

When I was a young minister, money was tight and I tried to manage it well. But against my better judgment and my gut instinct, I gave him the money.

Our relationship changed almost immediately. He didn't return my calls. He avoided me like I had leprosy. This went on for almost two years, and because we shared many of the same friends and lived in the same town, the awkwardness grew exponentially, especially if there was an event or a party we were both likely to attend, which happened several times. We wound up at the same concert once, and he managed to move around the room and avoid me the entire night. He actually left early, I assumed to avoid the inevitable awkwardness of me asking him for the money I'd loaned him. As time went on, what I had initially viewed as childish or mildly annoying behavior began to enrage me.

The situation consumed my thoughts every time I went for a run, cut the grass, took a shower, or went on a date with my girlfriend. I engaged in imaginary conversations with him, scenarios in which I told him off, sometimes with profanity and always in front of a crowd who cheered when I put him in his place. Occasionally I even dreamed about him. Sometimes in those dreams we fought, and when I punched him in the face, it felt good.

He owed me a debt I wanted him to repay. I couldn't get away from it. I couldn't let the thing go. Actually, it wouldn't let me go.

He owed me a debt I wanted him to repay. I couldn't get away from it. I couldn't let the thing go. Actually, it wouldn't let me go.

Truthfully, it wasn't the money I wanted. It was the satisfaction of knowing I hadn't let someone get the best of me. My pride was wounded, and I wanted to make him pay in order to prove that I was a better man than him.

The anger grew inside my heart like a malignant cancer. One night I dreamed he and I were arguing on a boat dock. He hit me with something, and we both fell in the water. We wrestled under the surface, and as I gripped the ladder to try to climb onto the dock, he grabbed my leg and pulled me back underwater. Multiple times I ascended the ladder, almost free of the water, only to have him pull me back under again. The dream ended as I grabbed his throat underwater, the realization flooding my mind, *He is trying to kill me and I need to drown him if I am going to live.*

When I awoke, I was sitting up in bed, wrapped in a web of sweaty sheets, staring into the darkness. Unable to shake off the remnants of the dream, I wandered downstairs into the living room. "This is insane," I said aloud to myself. "How did I wind up here? I can't go on like this. I have to let this thing go. I would rather forgive him than have this consume my thoughts. He can have the money. All I want is to move on."

I wrote those words in my journal early that morning. Then I wrote them on a piece of paper, addressed it to my old friend, stuck the letter in an envelope, placed a stamp on it, and drove it to the post office. It was still dark outside, and the world wouldn't wake up for another two hours, but my decision was made and I didn't want to wait a moment longer.

As soon as I dropped the letter into the mailbox, it was as if layers and layers of heavy, wet garments slid off my shoulders. I felt light, like I was floating in space. A feeling of euphoria swept through me when I realized I was finally free. My former friend couldn't control me anymore (even though he had no idea he was controlling me at all). The debt had no more power over me. It was forgiven. Just like Jesus had forgiven me, I was able to let this thing go.

I didn't know what my friend would do with the letter, or how he would receive it. Or whether he would continue to avoid me for the rest of his life. But that was on him, not me. I was free. Forgiveness really did bring freedom. And freedom is superior to slavery. Every single time.

To say this is difficult would be an understatement along the lines of saying that the *Titanic* took on a little bit of water. In fact, extending forgiveness is more than hard. It's impossible— unless you do it by God's grace through the power of the Holy Spirit. Jesus made this clear when he told Peter to forgive a brother or sister who had sinned against him not seven times but seventy-seven times (Matt. 18:22).

Peter thought he would impress Jesus by asking if he should forgive his neighbor seven times, since seven was a number of completion and wholeness for the Jews. Instead of affirming or rebuking Peter's attempt to impress him with his willingness to forgive more than once, Jesus taught Peter a lesson that I believe he wants to teach each of us, which is this: you won't just have to forgive one time. And when you think you've forgiven enough, it's still not sufficient. Seventy-seven times (or seventy times seven, according to some translations) symbolizes an infinite number, a never-ending number, a number with no end. In answering "not seven, but seventy-seven times," Jesus emphasized to Peter, and to us, that the act of forgiveness is ongoing. There is no end to forgiveness.

As long as you're living among sinners (i.e., human beings), they will offend and hurt you, and you will need to forgive them. As long as you're living in this broken world as a sinner, you will offend and hurt others, and you will need to be forgiven.

Under New Ownership

What an amazing gift! God gives us the power to move beyond offenses into a new reality, where we are controlled by the Holy Spirit rather than by the people who have hurt us. Looking back, we can often see how many years we wasted in refusing to forgive others as Jesus has forgiven us. Paul understood this all too well. Read what he said about the freedom Jesus gives to his followers:

> But thanks be to God that, though you used to be slaves to sin, you have come to obey from your heart the pattern of teaching that has now claimed your allegiance. You have been set free from sin and have become slaves to righteousness. . . . When you were slaves to sin, you were free from the control of righteousness. What benefit did you reap at that time from the things

you are now ashamed of? Those things result in death! But now that you have been set free from sin and have become slaves of God, the benefit you reap leads to holiness, and the result is eternal life. For the wages of sin is death, but the gift of God is eternal life in Christ Jesus our Lord. (Rom. 6:17–18, 20–23)

When you decide to forgive, no matter how hard it is or how long it takes, your old master loses control over you. You are under new ownership. Jesus sets you free to love people, to rest in his grace, and to forfeit the illusion of control. The sins of others don't dictate your mood anymore. You can go to bed in peace and wake up refreshed, living your daily life knowing that, because of the gospel, you can offer the same grace to others Jesus offers to you. The old way of living leads to death! Let Jesus set you free to forgive by remembering how he has forgiven you.

When you decide to forgive, no matter how hard it is or how long it takes, your old master loses control over you. You are under new ownership.

As Jesus hung on the cross, mere moments away from death, he prayed for his Father to forgive the very men who were murdering him. This same Jesus lives in the heart of Christians and compels us to extend the same forgiveness to those who do much less to us. Jesus not only set the example for us but also gives us the ability to overcome unforgiveness and to live out the very gospel that forgives us. His grace in us is the power we need to finally let go and forgive.

Get Started

Right after Sharie and I were married, I remember dropping a jar of honey on the tile floor in our kitchen. It didn't just break;

it exploded and seemed to multiply. Honey and broken glass went everywhere: under the refrigerator, in the grout between the tiles, on the cabinet doors, and all over my feet. I froze and looked at Sharie helplessly, as if to say, *What do I do? I've made the biggest mess in the history of the cosmos!* I must have looked so pathetic standing there, pitiful and paralyzed. What I really wanted was for her to work her female magic and start the cleaning process (I would have gladly assisted her . . . you know, if she needed it).

Your mind overrides your desire, because your long-term goals are more important than your current craving.

I'll never forget what she said: "Just pick a spot and get started."

When you're facing something as big and difficult as forgiving an offense, it's hard to know where to start because it all looks so daunting and impossible to overcome. I can't tell you how many times I've revisited Sharie's words when faced with what seemed like an insurmountable task. When it comes to forgiving someone, you just have to pick a spot and get started. Here are some tips for how to do exactly that.

Make the Decision

This process of forgiveness begins in the heart, but the heart and the mind have to work together. Your heart may be hurt, but your mind can override your emotions. In other words, you can decide to do the right thing, even if you don't feel like it. We do this all the time. You make yourself get out of bed and go to work or class even though you want to sleep in. You decide to skip dessert, go to the gym, and ignore the Krispy Kreme sign as you drive by. Why? Because you want to be healthy and live longer. Your mind overrides your desire, because your long-term goals are more important than your current craving. When your heart doesn't want to cooperate, choose to push through the negative feelings of fear and bitterness to make the decision that will put you on the path to peace and spiritual health. Decide to forgive, even if your feelings are telling you it's not possible. It is possible, so tell your feelings to shut up.

Say the Words

Proverbs 18:21 tells us that the power of life and death is in the tongue, and I've discovered this to be true in tangible, practical ways. No one spends more time with you than you do, so the one voice that has the greatest influence in your life is your own. Ask yourself, *What am I telling myself? What am I talking about?* You will believe what you tell yourself.

Once you choose to forgive, say it out loud. Not in your head—out loud, with words. Hear yourself say it over and over again: "I choose to forgive, and by God's grace, that is what I am going to do. Jesus forgave me so I can forgive them." Say it out loud, even when you don't believe it. And keep saying it until you do believe it.

Write It Down

When something is important, we write it down. We write down grocery lists, daily schedules, phone numbers, and names and dates to add to our calendar. If wise people had not taken the time to record important events, we wouldn't have the Bible or the stories of Jesus's life today.

We write things down to remember them but we also write things down for clarity. We say, "Get it in writing!" We do this precisely because when it's on paper, it's clear and not ambiguous.

Writing down your decision to forgive allows you the freedom to flesh out the process of forgiveness (and it is a process!). Journaling your journey is the best way to keep forward momentum. When you have a setback, write about it. When you struggle with the fact that the person you are forgiving still hasn't apologized or repented, write it down. When you spend an hour with your counselor trying to figure out how to stop hating your ex, write about it. You can even write out your prayers as you fight to stay free from the bitterness that used to consume you. When you write, you create a record, which you can return to in order to see proof of the progress you've made and celebrate how far Jesus has brought you.

And Repeat

It's likely you will have to repeat your initial decision to forgive over and over, perhaps for months or years. (Remember Jesus's words to Peter? Seventy-seven times.) Just when you least expect it, the memory of the offense will resurface, which in turn will resurrect feelings of anger and resentment. In this moment you will have a choice. You can choose to step back into the cesspool of toxic thoughts and poisonous memories and stay there. Or you can walk away from that temptation and continue to move forward.

If you need to, fall on your knees and pray out loud for God to strengthen you. Open your Bible and read a passage of Scripture out loud. Get your journal or a scrap of paper and write out a prayer or a statement of faith, such as, "I will not be taken back into slavery again. I will forgive! Jesus, help me. I'm struggling, but I will not give up the fight!" Don't isolate yourself. Call your pastor or a close friend to talk it out. Confess your weakness to a sister or brother and ask for advice or prayer. Read a book about the process of forgiveness.

· · · · · · · ·

Forgiveness is not easy. It's a slow and often painful process, but it ultimately leads to freedom and growth, godliness and joy . . . so you might as well keep walking it out.

Malcolm Graham lost a sister that night at Mother Emanuel Church in Charleston when Dylann Roof took the life of Cynthia Hurd, one of the nine murder victims. Mr. Graham does not gloss over the pain and anger he felt even as he listened to other family members speak about forgiving the killer. "Nine individual lives, families, faith walks. Some faith walks are longer than others. For me, forgiveness is a process," Graham continued. "It's a journey. Forgiving for me, then and now, is miles, miles, miles away."[6]

If you feel like forgiveness is miles away, then the best thing you can do is start moving. Pick a spot and get started.

Next Steps

The lie tells you that you can never be forgiven for the bad things you've done and that you can never forgive those who have done bad things to you. The truth is, God offers the gift of forgiveness, but you have to have faith to receive that gift.

None of us is *worthy* of the kind of love Jesus shows us, but each of us is *worth it*. That's why Jesus died in our place—because he values us and wants a relationship with us. Forgiveness removes the barriers that keep us from having good relationships with God and with others.

Going back to the previous section . . . why don't you pick a place and get started? Get concrete. I offer the following questions as a place to begin. Once you work through these, you will build momentum to keep moving forward toward forgiveness and freedom.

1. Is there an event from your past that you find yourself returning to over and over again in your mind? Identify it, then sit down and write it out; put as much of it down on paper as you can remember.

   ....

   ....

   ....

   ....

2. Is there one person in your life you could release from bitterness with a simple phone call and an apology for something that happened? Perhaps you made a hurtful comment, or the two of you have had a misunderstanding. Call that person and apologize. Try not to worry about their reaction. Make the first move.

   ....

   ....

   ....

   ....

3. Are you holding a grudge in your heart against someone who wronged or offended you? Write down their name and the offense. Then decide if you need to approach them about the offense or if you just need to let it go and forgive them in your own heart. This simple exercise may open your heart up to other offenses you didn't even know you were holding on to.

   ....

   ....

   ....

   ....

9

knocking on the door
to change

And Trusting God Will Answer

THE LIE: "I can never change."

THE TRUTH: True change is possible, and it begins with wanting to be well.

> I write to you, dear children, because you know the Father. I write to you, fathers, because you know him who is from the beginning. I write to you, young men, because you are strong, and the word of God lives in you, and you have OVERCOME the evil one.
>
> 1 John 2:14

Before this book was a real book, as in actual words on the page or screen, it was just a concept, an idea birthed in my mind as the result of a conversation with a friend. He had thrown in the towel, as they say. He'd completely given up on pretty much everything that constituted his life. After several failed marriages, numerous run-ins with the law, nearly two decades of substance abuse, and even a few unsuccessful suicide attempts, he had come to the conclusion that he was damaged goods. He was too old to turn things around, and it didn't really matter anyway. I clearly remember the conversation we shared as I attempted to convince him to keep fighting.

"You've got so many good years ahead of you," I pleaded. "You're still young, not even in your late thirties. You have children who adore you and just want you to be their daddy. If you would just decide that you want to change, to make something out of yourself, you could turn things around right now."

Those words sounded reasonable as they left my mouth. I also believed them to be true. But he didn't.

"What's the use in trying?" he argued. "Look at me. I'm a drunk. I haven't had a real job in years. My kids know when I'm using [a reference to his drug addiction] and a good woman will never want to date me. The only ones I attract are the kind that just want to use me, because when the good ones find out what kind of guy I am, they run away. I don't blame them. I'd run away from me too. Maybe that's what I was trying to do when I tried to kill myself—run away from who I am. But I can't. I am who I am and there's no changing for me. You can't teach an old dog new tricks." Then, cigarette dangling from his lips, he opened another beer.

I sat across from him, staring in sad disbelief. Addiction is such a cruel disease. An able-bodied young man with unlimited potential born in the richest culture that has ever existed with opportunities for education, employment, and health care that billions of other humans on earth could only dream of . . . and he was chucking it all into the garbage because he had made up his mind. He would never change. And that was that.

I left that conversation filled with anger, yet I was determined not to let my frustration cycle fruitlessly around in my head. I decided to externalize the negative emotions I was feeling by writing them down. Here's what I wrote that day shortly after leaving one of the most discouraging conversations of my life:

People are creatures of habit, and once habits are formed and reinforced, they become "habitual" and hard to break. It's easier to believe that you can never change than it is to do the hard work of self-assessment and self-correction. Small decisions become habits and habits become patterns and patterns turn into addictions. I remember hearing a youth pastor when I was a teenager say, "You sow a thought, you reap an action. You sow an action, you reap a habit. You sow a habit, you reap a lifestyle. You sow a lifestyle, you reap your destiny."

Before you know it, you've become enslaved to insecurity, bitterness, pornography, prescription pills, binge eating, cutting and self-harm, or abusive relationships . . . all the while telling yourself that you can never break free of the chains that hold you down. This lie is rooted in the fear of facing the hard truth about yourself: that you are messed up and need to work on your junk. We don't really want to change because we're afraid of doing the hard work of owning our own dysfunction and sin. The truth is, you can change, but not on your own. You need a power greater than yourself to knock off the shackles of shame, and that power is the gospel of Jesus Christ, which promises you can be made new and whole through confession, repentance, and restoration. That's the whole essence of the gospel; everyone can change, no matter who they are or what they've done. I wish

I could convince my friend [name withheld] of this. But until the misery of his current situation surpasses the fear of facing his own mistakes and shame, he won't change.

Should I pray for him to hit rock bottom? Is that a bad thing to ask God for? Because it looks like that's what it's going to take. How low would rock bottom be for him? How ugly and painful would things have to get for him to actually want to change?

There you have it: the genesis of this book, the root source of this idea that we all believe lies that hold us down. It's not just a theory. It's reality, but we can change our reality.

There is a way out. We can change. We can overcome this lie and the fear it creates in us.

I've seen it up close and personal. I've had a front-row seat and a backstage pass.

A Front-Row Seat

As a music enthusiast, I used to love going to live shows. My first concert was (this is a confession, not a testimony) Hank Williams Jr. That's right, the living legend of country music himself who made millions singing about being "whiskey bent and hell bound." Three things stand out to me about my first concert: (1) I knew I never wanted to get drunk; (2) I would later preach the gospel in that same auditorium to thousands of people, proving that God has a great sense of humor; and (3) I fell in love with big concerts.

After the opening song at that Hank Williams Jr. concert, I knew one thing for sure: I would never be happy in the nosebleed section. I wanted a front-row seat! A few years later, after I'd become a Christian and begun listening to Christian music, my ambition was finally realized: I got a front-row seat at a Petra concert. Oh boy, did that change my life! I didn't think anything could top that experience.

I'm going somewhere with this. Each of us has a front-row seat to the lives of others. We see them make bad choices, dating the wrong people, spending money indiscriminately, picking terrible friends. We watch them as they hurtle down a destructive road. We warn them. We reason with them. We pray for them. We know where things are headed because we have a front-row seat, and a front-row seat has perspective. It gets you close up, close enough to see what's happening—and what will happen.

Each of us also has a front-row seat to our own lives. No one is closer to you than you are. No one spends more time with you than you do. Yet so many of us don't pay attention to the things we do or the choices we make.

Each of us also has a front-row seat to our own lives. No one is closer to you than you are. No one spends more time with you than you do. Yet so many of us don't pay attention to the things we do or the choices we make. We have a front-row seat to our own lives but we simply observe the show, mindlessly detached from the actual action that's taking place.

Sitting on the porch that day with my friend, I couldn't wrap my mind around how disconnected he was from his own life. We both had a front-row seat, but it seemed I was the only one actually watching the show. I knew he could change. I could see it. I knew it would take time, discipline, surrender, hard work, and even some setbacks, but I knew he could do it. But he wouldn't listen to me. He wouldn't let me in.

I had a front-row seat, but what I needed was a backstage pass.

A Backstage Pass

When I was sixteen, my local Christian bookstore held a contest to give away backstage passes for one of my favorite Christian rock bands, which was scheduled to perform in nearby Spartanburg. I entered the contest (sixty-seven times) and I won! The afternoon of the concert, I drove to the venue and was escorted into the dressing room from a special parking lot in the back. I walked into the auditorium where the band would play, and I literally sat on the side of the stage. A few minutes later, the band members all walked on stage together and began playing their instruments for a sound check. After twenty minutes of mundane, random notes and runs, the musicians, without a word spoken between them, seamlessly tore into a song. It sounded exactly like it was coming from my car stereo, but it was alive, it was close, and the song was being created right there on the stage in front of me. These guys were making music in real time, and it simply blew my mind.

They blazed through their set list, and the more they played, the more fascinated I became. When they were done, their manager walked me over to them, on the stage, guitars still strapped on their shoulders, and introduced me. They invited me backstage, where we sat at a huge table and ate dinner. These guys were larger than life to me, but there I was, talking with them like normal people would talk. They were kind, funny, and engaging as they chatted with me about how the band was formed, how they wrote and recorded songs, the challenges of touring, and how they handled conflicts that arose between them.

When the show started later that evening, I was far more connected to the entire experience than the rest of the fans in the audience. Why? Because I'd had a backstage pass, and that pass had given me the two things no one else had.

First, it gave me *access*. I had already been as close as someone could get to the band that day. I watched them play their entire set while standing a few feet away from them. I was the only other person in the room. I sat across a table from them as we ate dinner together. I watched them tune their guitars backstage.

Second, it gave me *understanding*. I knew the backstory of how the band members came to faith in Christ and how their love for music translated into their calling to play for God's glory. I knew some of what went into writing, recording, rehearsing, and touring. I saw the whole setup before the doors opened. I understood the experience.

So many of us look at our current situation, with all its frustrations and problems, and think to ourselves, *I've been here for so long; this is just how it is and this is just who I am. I will never change. I might as well live with it.* That's the way an observer thinks. That's the attitude of someone who paid for a front-row seat. They're happy to sit there and watch, but there is no personal involvement, no connection.

Is that how you're approaching the things in your life that need to change? Have you fallen for the lie that there's nothing you can do about your situation? Have you already decided this is how things are going to be forever? Because if that describes you and your attitude, you've already conceded defeat. But you don't have to stay defeated—maybe what you need is to move from the front row to backstage. It's a whole different world back there.

So Close You Can Touch It

When I was twelve, the Hank Williams Jr. concert was the most amazing experience in the world. Or so I thought. Then I got to sit in the front row at a Petra concert. I thought absolutely nothing could top that! Little did I know there was another level that far superseded the front-row experience.

My backstage pass had a dramatic impact on my life. As a result of that experience, I eventually started not one but two bands. We recorded seven records, toured the East Coast, sold over ten thousand CDs, and played on stage with Third Day and Jars of Clay. But our greatest moment came when a band of young, blond surfer dudes from southern California opened up for us at a concert near Charlotte, North Carolina, a few years after I graduated college. That band was Switchfoot. Yep, Switchfoot opened up for us. (Drops the mic, walks off stage).

What if you quit believing the lie that it's too hard to change, and you had access—a backstage pass, if you will—to something that proved to you that you could get better?

Until that backstage experience, I had always loved music and was an okay singer, but I never dreamed of picking up an instrument, forming a band, or writing a song. Those things seemed too hard, far beyond my capabilities. But something clicked in me that night backstage. I saw it was possible. I began dreaming of doing it myself. The *access* to those band members and the behind-the-scenes experience was a game-changer for me. The *understanding* I gained from the experience showed me it wasn't too hard. It was possible.

What if you quit believing the lie that it's too hard to change, and you had access—a backstage pass, if you will—to something that proved to you that you could get better? And what if that access gave you a completely new level of understanding, a perspective that you had never considered before, allowing you to finally break free of the things you thought would never change?

It's not just possible. It's tangible. It's so close that you can touch it.

When You Feel Like the Door Is Closed and Locked

You have access to the greatest power in the entire universe. Stronger than any military or government, more powerful than any energy force or weapon of mass destruction, the unlimited and unfathomable power of God is at your disposal. The same power that could overcome the grave is available to you. That power is not an independent entity, however. It's not something you can purchase or barter for. The power of God is a byproduct of God himself, and it cannot exist apart from him. In other words, if you want to experience the power of God to change you, you have to know the God who possesses that power. You can't get his power except by getting him. A relationship with God is the way you access his power, but it's not a means to an end. The relationship is the end itself.

The enemy doesn't want you to know you have access to God. He lies to you and tries to convince you that a relationship with God is out of your reach. *That's for religious professionals who have their junk together,* he whispers. *That's for good people with nice clothes who know how to dress for church. That's for people with money and success who know how to get things done and be rewarded by God for their hard work.*

The enemy lies to you again and again, telling you that you can never overcome the things you need to change because you can never really be close to God. If you listen to these lies, you begin to believe that God is like a superstar you watch from a distance—detached, doing his thing up there in heaven like a rock star does his thing up on stage. The best thing you can hope for is a seat in the audience, watching the show take place. But you'll never actually get to meet him. Or talk to him. Or know him.

This is the lie. The fear that fuels this lie tells you that if you try to change, you will fail and become a failure. It takes you from a verb to a noun. Failing is not just what you do. It is who you are.

This is the lie. The fear that fuels this lie tells you that if you try to change, you will fail and become a failure. It takes you from a verb to a noun. Failing is not just what you do. It is who you are.

If the enemy can lie to you and convince you that you don't have access to God, then you assume you can never know God and thus never have an understanding of who God is and who you really are in relationship to him. This seems to be the great dilemma of our day: people believe in God but don't know what he's really like or how they can get to know him personally. It's one thing to believe God exists. It's quite another thing to feel like he's approachable, like you can really understand him and he can understand you. Because if that were possible, you really could change, right? But it doesn't matter when you feel like the door between you and God is locked and you can't get in.

The Door Is Unlocked

During the process of writing this book, my family built a house. Truth be told, we didn't do most of the building. We paid some guys to do it. And as a bit of free advice, I'd suggest you strongly consider *not* adding any extra projects to your life during the construction of a new home. Like writing a book . . . but I digress.

For months people came and went at the construction site. We never knew when they would show up. There were painters and plumbers, electricians and carpenters, and everyone had a key to the house. This was a good thing, so long as we were still living off-site in an apartment. But once we moved into the house, we had to change the locks so the crew of cabinet installers couldn't walk in on me in my underwear making coffee on a Saturday morning (not that I would ever do that).

So we changed the locks but we didn't get a spare key. We intended to get a key-code lock installed on the garage door, but the installation was delayed. We didn't think we needed a spare key . . . until we needed a spare key.

When we returned home one day after running some errands, I realized I'd left the house key inside. My kids had locked the garage door as they left, just as we had trained them to do. I tried it anyway, and when it wouldn't open, I knew we were locked out. What frustrated me the most was that it was my fault.

Nothing irritates me more than being locked out of my own car or my own house. They're mine! I paid for them. I should be able to have access to them anytime. Why can't someone invent a biometric scanner that's embedded in every car door and house door that can scan my fingerprint or the cornea of my eye (or the pores on my nose, for that matter) so that I'm never locked out? They have those in the movies. Someone get on that, please.

When I realized we were locked out, my blood pressure shot up, my body temperature skyrocketed, and the panic escalated to DEFCON 1. I seriously thought about throwing a rock through a window (to get inside and also to blow off some steam). The garage door was locked. The back porch door was locked. The bedroom door was locked. The side door was locked. The windows were locked. Everything was locked, and I was blocked and my temper was cocked (sometimes when I retell a story I relive the emotion and I rhyme. Just so you know).

As I was praying for patience (I didn't want to lose it in front of my kids and throw the kind of tantrum I was always telling them they shouldn't throw), it hit me: I hadn't checked the front door.

It was a long shot. We always locked the front door. It faces the road, allowing the easiest access to potential criminals. This door was never, ever unlocked.

Opening the door isn't the hard part. The hard part is believing the door is open for you.

I slowly walked up the steps and across the porch, grabbed the door handle, and—you guessed it, the front door swung open with ease. The front door had been unlocked the entire time. I had assumed the house was out of reach, but the door was wide open for us. We simply had to reach out and open it, and we were able to walk directly into the house.

That's how it is with God. The door into his house and into his heart is always unlocked; we simply have to reach out and open it. Opening the door isn't the hard part. The hard part is believing the door is open for you.

When you feel like the door has been slammed in your face and your failures and sins have made you unlovable and unforgivable, God tells you he hasn't cast you out on the street. When the lies accumulate one after the other, reminding you of the times you've been hurt, betrayed, disappointed, and deceived, he has more grace for you! It never runs out. When you feel accused, condemned from the unrelenting lying voices inside your head, the door to a better life is open and unlocked. As James reminds us:

> He gives us more grace. That is why Scripture says,
>
> > "God opposes the proud
> > but shows favor to the humble."
>
> Submit yourselves, then, to God. Resist the devil, and he will flee from you. *Come near to God and he will come near to you.* (James 4:6–8, emphasis added)

Now that is truly a beautiful promise.

As long as you are humble enough to come to him for help, to call on him for grace, he will be there waiting. The door is not locked. It's wide open, and inside is God, lovingly waiting on you to cross the threshold. Come near to God and you will find him coming near to you, already looking your way, already heading in your direction, longing to embrace you, his child. Change begins when you open the door to God.

Do You Want to Change?

Some years ago I was eating a meal with a group of friends, and I listened as someone at the table rattled on about how hard it was for him to wake up early enough to get to the gym. He also complained that it was incredibly difficult for him to stop using his credit card (he had just maxed out another card and admitted he was about $10,000 in credit card debt). Finally he declared, "I guess I'm just too old to change. I'm stuck in my ways and maybe I'll always be this undisciplined slob of a man. It's just too hard to change."

Sitting at the same table was a young lady who evidently knew the man (at least I hope she did, considering how she responded to his comment about his inability to change). "Come on, that's a load of bull," she admonished. "You're a grown man. Act like it. You're talking like a middle-schooler. Getting up early isn't hard. Paying off debt isn't hard. Give me a break! Living with cancer is hard. Kicking a heroin addiction is hard. Losing a child is hard. The stuff you're dealing with isn't hard. You're just lazy and you don't want to change."

Her approach was blunt, to say the least. At the same time, though, it was refreshing to hear someone cut through the self-pitying nonsense and call things what they were. I looked at the guy. He sat motionless, frozen by the brutal truth uttered by this bold, brave young woman. I said to him, "You should marry her. Or at least ask her out."

Anyone can change. Honestly. Listen to someone whine about how hard it is to overcome a bad habit, like sleeping late or spending too much money or drinking too much or overeating. Isn't it often hard to refrain from saying what you really want to say? It's so simple to see how easy it would be for *others* to change, but so hard for us to believe we can change. Or that we need to overcome that thing that has overpowered us.

You can become so used to the way things are that you don't want to even think about the way things could be.

The simple truth is this: some people who need to change don't want to change. The familiarity of destructive patterns, the close proximity of toxic people and bad relationships, the ease of doing what we've always done, and the ingrained habits of self-medicating to escape from hard reality—all these factors and more keep many of us locked into ways of thinking and existing that rob us of the joy of being alive! You can become so used to the way things are that you don't want to even think about the way things could be. Before you know it, decades of your life have passed you by, and when you look back all you feel is regret.

There is a way out. You *can* overcome, but first you have to own what's yours.

Do You Want to Get Well?

I've been to some pretty depressing places in my life, but few rival the psychiatric ward at a regional hospital I visited one afternoon. A friend had battled addiction for years and was locked in the only safe place available to him after he had lost everything but the clothes on his back.

Family and friends could visit their loved ones once a week, for thirty minutes on Sunday afternoons. Dozens of us crowded into a large room. Orderlies and staff lined the walls and security officers stood in the shadows, Taser guns in hand in case things took an unexpected turn for the worse. The mood in the room was somewhere between somber and sorrowful. For many, the psychiatric ward was the last place they could go before they wound up walking the streets, destitute, sleeping under a bridge or in an abandoned building.

When my friend arrived at the table, he looked subdued and resigned. For several decades, drugs had been his master and he had been their slave. His life had become a web of lies and deception, blame and bitterness, seasons of sobriety followed by suicidal drug binges that lasted for weeks. The people who loved him had spent thousands of dollars to fund detox clinics, rehab, automobiles, free rent, clothing, and medical costs.

Nothing helped. The reason was simple: until that point, he hadn't wanted to change.

After a few minutes of small talk (there's only so much superficiality in the psych ward), he opened up with a bold transparency. "Clayton, I am not going to ask you for any help," he said. "The only thing I want to ask you for today is forgiveness. I'm sorry for the times I took advantage of you and all the other people who tried to help me. I wasted so much time and money. But now that I have nothing, I think I finally want to get help. I really want to change this time. I don't want to die. I want to live. I did all of this to myself and now I have to own up to it."

I have to own up to it. Finally, it seemed, he really wanted to overcome.

For him, like so many who have fought for their lives in a war with substance abuse and addiction, that was the turning point. Professional counselors all know that until someone wants to change, nothing can change them. Pastors figure this out about their church members, coaches know this about their players, teachers know it's true of their students, and parents understand this truth about their children.

Ultimately, God knows it too.

We have to want to change in order to change. We must have a desire to get better, to be free, to get well, to get on with life. It seems even Jesus knew this when he asked a crippled man a simple question one day:

> Some time later, Jesus went up to Jerusalem for one of the Jewish festivals. Now there is in Jerusalem near the Sheep Gate a pool, which in Aramaic is called Bethesda and which is surrounded by five covered colonnades. Here a great number of disabled people used to lie—the blind, the lame, the paralyzed. One

who was there had been an invalid for thirty-eight years. When Jesus saw him lying there and learned that he had been in this condition for a long time, he asked him, *"Do you want to get well?"* (John 5:1–6, emphasis added)

What a horrible, offensive question! How could Jesus be so insensitive to this poor man? Was the man offended by Jesus's insinuation that he may not actually want to get well? Jesus didn't seem to be very concerned with hurting the man's feelings. He wanted to shake the man out of his hopelessness, the place he had been stranded for nearly forty years.

How many people had told the man to give up, to stop trying, to live in reality, to accept the way things were? This is how lies work; they relentlessly attack us to keep us from hoping for a better life. They accumulate, one on top of another, until they drown out the truth.

Predictably, the lie follows the same pattern once again. It *infiltrates* your mind as a simple thought or a comment made by someone close to you, and you can't shake the idea that maybe your current condition is your ultimate conclusion. Things will never get better.

Then the lie *insinuates* that you're powerless to move forward because you're a weakling without the ability to help yourself. It tells you to look back at your past, at your own personal version of the invalid's thirty-eight-year saga. You've always drunk too much and you can't stop now. You've been insecure about your body image since you were a kid and you will be until you die. It whispers that your history is your destiny.

Next the lie *intimidates* you by telling you that any effort to get well will fail. You will fall flat on your face if you try to lose thirty pounds or attempt to fix your marriage. It'll be too embarrassing to try counseling for your depression, and you'll quit after two months. You can't read the Bible every day because it's too hard and too confusing. Besides, you tried it four years ago and bailed after a week.

Finally the lie *re-creates* your reality until you believe that any effort to change would just be wasted energy. You give up and give in. You're too old to get in shape. You're too stubborn to apologize and restore the broken relationship with your parents. You don't make enough money to get out of debt. You tell yourself to get used to the way things are because that's how they're going to be. Forever. You begin to live in the new reality the lie re-created for you. And you stay stuck.

Does this describe you? Fatigued from your failure, worn out from worrying, tired of trying . . . but somehow still hanging on? That's a good thing!

Maybe you've lost hope. Maybe you've all but given up and given in to what feels like the inevitable. But don't miss one small detail in this Bible story: the crippled man hadn't walked in thirty-eight years, yet there he was, sitting by the healing pool. He was still showing up, day after day after day, perhaps simply out of habit, hoping somehow for a miracle. Does this describe you? Fatigued from your failure, worn out from worrying, tired of trying . . . but somehow still hanging on? That's a good thing!

It's easy for us to get used to dysfunction and sympathy. Although this man may have said he wanted to be healed, inside he may have secretly succumbed to what he assumed was the inevitable. *I've been like this for thirty-eight years*, he may have told himself. *Things will never change.*

But things did change once the man met Jesus. They changed with one simple question: *Do you want to get well?*

That question was Jesus's way of lovingly calling the man to a place of decision. Of course the invalid could no more heal himself than he could sprout wings and fly, but Jesus stirred something up in the man that had all but died as he suffered decade after decade of disease and disability. Jesus's question stirred up faith in the man, faith that had perhaps long lain dormant. Jesus's question resurrected his faith—faith that he could change, faith that things could be different.

> "Sir," the invalid replied, "I have no one to help me into the pool when the water is stirred. While I am trying to get in, someone else goes down ahead of me."
> Then Jesus said to him, "Get up! Pick up your mat and walk." At once the man was cured; he picked up his mat and walked. (vv. 7–9)

Jesus's question was a call to action, forcing the man to decide if he really wanted a way out of his predicament. Jesus then listened to the man's explanation of why he believed his situation was hopeless. Perhaps the invalid was telling the truth. Perhaps he truly believed there was no conceivable way he'd ever walk with his own two legs. But it's also just as likely this was the excuse the man had relied on for years. The man did not need a bath in the healing pool; he needed a supernatural touch from God. When he couldn't make it on his own, Jesus came to him and removed not only the excuse but also the sickness. Jesus healed him and he walked, for the first time in almost forty years. He was changed.

Do you want to change? Do you want to be well? Do you need a second chance, a gigantic do-over? You'll need Someone bigger and stronger than you to do it for you, just like the discouraged paralytic who had a valid excuse to stay crippled for the rest of his life. When you meet Jesus, there are no more excuses. Like sunlight burns off the morning fog, Jesus burns away any excuse to stay stuck where you are. He can help you. He will help you. He is your way out.

Ask, Seek, Knock

The action you must take is actually quite simple. It requires minimal effort but maximum faith. You have to believe the door is unlocked. You have to believe that if you knock, the door will open for you.

> Ask and it will be given to you; seek and you will find; knock and the door will be opened to you. For everyone who asks receives; the one who seeks finds; and to the one who knocks, the door will be opened. (Matt. 7:7–8)

These words are not merely symbolic. They are Jesus's concrete promises that we can plant our feet on and build our lives on. This is the way to change. We walk toward God. We move in his direction. We humble ourselves, admitting we are powerless to change on our own. We ask for help in prayer. And we knock on the door. We keep knocking, believing that God will not pretend he isn't home, believing he will open the door and invite us into a deeper relationship with him, where we rely on his strength in our weakness.

You have to believe the door is unlocked. You have to believe that if you knock, the door will open for you.

That's the first step. After that, change can look very different depending on your circumstances. The journey toward complete transformation may require counseling, rehab, detox, support groups, therapy, a new job, selling the house you can't afford, breaking off a relationship, changing churches, losing weight, returning to church, new eating habits, new sleeping habits, a new exercise routine, or a more disciplined spiritual life . . . you get the idea. But remember, none of these practices can change you without God. His Spirit, the Holy Spirit who lives inside of you, is the change agent:

> Therefore, if anyone is in Christ, the new creation has come: The old has gone, the new is here! (2 Cor. 5:17)

The value of something isn't based on markets, charts, graphs, or economic trends. The value of something is based completely on what someone is willing to pay for it. Are you willing to pay for the change you want to see? Are you willing to surrender in trust to Christ? Will you invest the energy and the self-discipline? If you really value the change you know you need to make, you will pay whatever it costs to see it happen.

Perhaps the best thing you can do right now is put down this book and start talking to God, out loud if you have to. Carve out some time by yourself, find a private place, and ask him for help. Seek his face. Knock on his door. Go to him. No matter what burdens you carry, no matter what struggles you face, he is waiting for you, and his deepest desire is to help you change, to be transformed into a new creation and made new. Jesus said, "I have given you authority to trample on snakes and scorpions and to overcome all the power of the enemy; nothing will harm you" (Luke 10:19).

Next Steps

To be human is to be broken, and each of us has areas where we need real change to occur. Admitting this is the first step toward health and wholeness, restored relationships, and even intimacy with God.

Let's get specific and name the issues you struggle with and the areas where you need to grow, repent, learn, abandon, delete, or begin.

1. Name three bad habits that are hurting you or your relationships in some way.

....

....

....

....

2. How would you rate your overall physical health? Specifically, how is your weight and your exercise routine?

....

....

....

....

3. How do you sleep at night? What are your anxiety levels like?

....

....

....

....

4. Is there anything in your life that you would say you are addicted to (or borderline addicted to)? Is there anything you can't stop doing that you know is destructive?

....

....

....

....

5. Compare the time you spend in prayer, reading Scripture, worship, and intentional community with other Christians to the
   amount of time you spend on social media (Facebook, Instagram,
   Twitter, Snapchat, etc.). What might this tell you about yourself?

....

....

....

....

6. Who could you ask right now to help you change in the areas
   where you know you need to? Write their name(s) here and commit to ask them within the next forty-eight hours to help you.

....

....

....

....

10

live and love again

Allowing the Truth to Set You Free

> For everyone born of God OVERCOMES the world. This is the victory that has OVERCOME the world, even our faith.
>
> 1 John 5:4

The lies we listen to are leading us somewhere, and the destination is always destruction. The truth takes us to a better place, but we won't get there unless we learn to recognize the lies when we hear them and the fears underneath.

I checked my Facebook messages early one morning. I have a public figure page, which works a little differently than a regular Facebook account, and I admit that I don't read and respond to all my messages as promptly as some do. As I scrolled the page, one message caught my attention. As the words unfolded on the screen, I realized I was reading a story not only about the power of lies to fill us with fear but also about how the truth overcomes the lies—because the truth is always stronger.

Hi Clayton; you are the pastor at Newspring Church and I just wanted to say thank you so much for everything you do and the gospel that is preached at our church. I just moved to the coast of South Carolina several months ago from another state. I was not living a good life. I was an exotic dancer. I struggled every day with drinking and drugs, and I was taking pills to cope with the fact that I didn't want to be there. I believed that it was the only way I could make money because I never graduated from high school. Also, my mother and father are not in my life at all. My dad is an alcoholic and my mom is a drug addict.

I was so lost and down that I had multiple instances where I thought about suicide. Finally, my boyfriend and I decided to move and try to start over. We both agreed we needed to find different jobs. I was hired at a new place where I was able to meet new people and interact with them all day at work. We knew we needed to find a church, and one day I was talking about it at work when a customer told me about her church. She pulled up the Newspring app on her phone. She showed me some of the sermons there and invited me to church. I said yes, and I went, and it was awesome! I couldn't wait to go back. The next Sunday during the sermon I was so moved, I kept getting goose bumps the whole time during the message and it made total sense to me.

At the invitation I stood up and I was singing and crying and I thought someone was whispering to me so I opened my eyes and saw everyone else singing too. Then I heard the Lord say to me that it was time to give my life to him. Right then and there I walked out the aisle and toward the back of the auditorium where I prayed with someone and gave everything to Jesus.

I was baptized the next Sunday and now I just feel so extremely blessed! I just wanted to tell you how thankful I am for how the Lord has changed me. I look forward to going to church every Sunday now so I can hear the gospel and feel loved and accepted.

I read the message a second time. I didn't want to miss any detail. This is the kind of thing I live for! This woman's life had been changed; she had been rescued from darkness and despair. As I read and reread her testimony, I saw it clearly. I saw the lie that had been holding her down: "I believed that it was the only way I could make money because I never graduated from high school."

The lie had *infiltrated* her mind, *insinuated* that she wasn't smart enough to make something of herself because she didn't graduate from high school, *intimidated* her into believing that she had to take her clothes off for money just to survive, and *re-created* her identity as a woman burdened by the shame of her occupation and the pain of her past.

There was a second lie as well: "Also, my mother and father are not in my life at all. My dad is an alcoholic and my mom is a drug addict." Do you remember the lie I confessed at the beginning of the book, that I would always be alone and unloved? I felt that familiar fear when I read her words again. She felt alone. Unloved. Abandoned. Isolated. She had no support from her parents, the very people who were supposed to love her the most and believe the best about her. Can you imagine the lies running through her mind and the fear they produced in her heart?

In the midst of the lies that controlled her, God reached out to her. She felt an ache in her heart to be free of the bondage she was living in, and in his sovereignty God moved her and her boyfriend to a new town, where she got a new job and made a new friend who invited her to a new church. She went to that new church and heard a new message of how God could make her a new person. She became a Christian. She received forgiveness for her sins and began to follow Christ.

The truth had replaced the lies. She was not damaged goods. Her history did not have to be her destiny. Her current condition was not her ultimate conclusion. She could be liberated from shame and guilt. Faith replaced fear, and she changed direction when she repented of her sins and received the love of Jesus.

But the best part of this story is what happened on a recent Sunday morning.

We have seventeen campuses across South Carolina, but I preach from our central campus, where we have multiple services on Sunday. The first service happens at 9:15 a.m., and that's the sermon we record and play at all of our other campuses all day long and even on Sunday night. As I prepared my message for that day, I knew her story would have a deep spiritual impact on our church community, so with her permission and her real name withheld, I printed out her testimony and read it at the end of the service. Our church is very evangelistic, so when we hear stories of how the gospel changes lives, we go crazy. People began to clap and shout, celebrating how Jesus had found this young woman and turned her life around. Then I invited anyone who was broken and far from God to give their lives to Christ, just like she had done, and to repent of their sin and trust Jesus for salvation.

Sixteen other campuses from across our state were watching the message, and I anticipated that many would respond to the gospel. But I didn't expect what I heard just fifteen minutes after I extended the invitation.

Eric came to find me backstage. He is a gigantic man, what I imagine Goliath looked like. He works on our security team and has a tender heart for the Lord. "Clayton, you are not gonna believe this!" Eric shouted. "You know the lady you were talking about? The one who just got saved and baptized and set free from drugs and exotic dancing?"

Umm, yeah, I know . . . I just told her story.

"Well, she was sitting in the audience just now, at one of our other campuses on the other side of the state. And her boyfriend was sitting beside her. As soon as you invited people to give their lives to Jesus, he stood straight up and walked out the back and met with a care team member, and he just gave his life to Jesus too."

That's how the truth works! When the lie is exposed, it begins to lose all control over you. Its death grip on your life starts to slip away and the truth begins to take root. You can begin to breathe again, to live again. To love again.

You are not unloved. God loves you.

You are not alone. God's Spirit is always with you.

You are not without hope, even when you feel out of control. Jesus can stop the spin cycle.

Your suffering is not meaningless. God will use your pain to transform you and others.

Your body is not worthless. God made you in his image, and he values your body and your soul.

You are not at the mercy of temptation. The Holy Spirit empowers you to stand firm.

You do not need wealth to be secure. Your Savior offers you complete security.

It's not impossible to forgive or be forgiven. Jesus proved it on the cross.

You're not destined to stay stuck. You can change by the power of God's grace.

Can you feel it? Can you feel the lies losing their grip on you? Can you sense a shift taking place in your heart as the truth breaks through the darkness and shines light into your soul? Can you feel yourself overcoming the lies that overpower you and the fear that overwhelms you?

Can you feel yourself overcoming the lies that overpower you and the fear that overwhelms you?

The tiniest truth breaks the biggest lie. Now imagine what it's like not just to taste the truth but to feast on it! Imagine your mind, your heart, your relationships, your entire life filled with what God says instead of what the lies say. That is the life God wants for you, the life Jesus died to give you, the life you have always wanted.

This is how you overcome. Jesus said, "The thief comes only to steal and kill and destroy; I have come that they may have life, and have it to the full" (John 10:10).

notes

Chapter 1 Getting to Know the Real God

1. A. W. Tozer, *The Knowledge of the Holy* (Nashville: Harper One, 2009), 23.

Chapter 4 Understanding the Purpose of Suffering

1. Shannon Evans, "How Suffering Saved My Faith," *Relevant*, November 5, 2015, relevantmagazine.com/god/practical-faith/how-suffering-saved-my-faith.
2. Ibid.
3. Ibid.

Chapter 5 Love and Intimacy

1. Joe McIlhaney, MD, and Freda McKissic Bush, MD, *Hooked: New Science on How Casual Sex Is Affecting Our Children* (Chicago: Northfield Publishers, 2008), 45.
2. Ibid., 137.
3. Ibid., 100–101, emphasis added.
4. O. Arias-Carrion and E. Poppel, "Dopamine, Learning and Reward-Seeking Behavior," *Acta Neurobiologiae Expermintalis* 67, no. 4 (2007): 481–88.
5. McIlhaney and Bush, *Hooked*, 39.
6. Ibid., 37.
7. Ibid., 43.
8. Joan R. Kahn and Kathryn A. London, "Premarital Sex and the Risk of Divorce," *Journal of Marriage and the Family* 53 (November 1991): 845–55.
9. Ibid., 882–83.

10. Danice K. Eaton et al., "Youth Risk Behavior Surveillance: United States, 2005," *MMWR Surveillance Summaries,* June 9, 2006, https://www.cdc.gov/mmwr/preview/mmwrhtml/ss5505a1.htm.

11. Kahn and London, "Premarital Sex and the Risk of Divorce," 845–55.

12. R. Finger et al., "Association of Virginity at Age 18 with Educational Economic, Social and Health Outcomes in Middle Adulthood," *Adolescent and Family Health* 3, no. 4 (2004): 164–70.

13. Edward Laumann, Robert T. Michael, and Gina Kolata, *Sex in America* (New York: Time Warner, 1995), 127.

14. McIlhaney and Bush, *Hooked,* 77.

15. Ari Fleischer, "How to Fight Income Inequality: Get Married," *The Wall Street Journal,* January 12, 2014, m.us.wsj.com/articles/SB100014240 5270230432500457929675240487761 2?mg=reno64-wsj.

16. John A. T. Robinson, *The Body: A Study in Pauline Theology* (London: SCM, 1955), 9, emphasis added.

17. Lauren F. Winner, *Real Sex: The Naked Truth about Chastity* (Grand Rapids: Brazos Press, 2005), 37, emphasis added.

18. Ibid.

19. Ibid.

Chapter 6   Fighting Temptation with Faith

1. Walter Mischel, *The Marshmallow Test: Mastering Self Control* (New York: Little, Brown and Company, 2014).

2. "Delaying Gratification," American Psychological Association, accessed October 18, 2016, www.apa.org/helpcenter//willpower-gratification.pdf.

Chapter 7   The Pursuit of Happiness

1. Summary and details of Jack Whittaker's story from April Witt, "Rich Man, Poor Man," *The Washington Post,* January 30, 2005, www.washingtonpost.com/wp-dyn/articles/A36338-2005Jan25.html, unless otherwise noted.

2. Martin Bashir and Sara Holmberg, "Powerball Winner Says He's Cursed," *ABC News,* April 6, 2007, abcnews.go.com/2020/powerball-winner-cursed/story?id=3012631.

3. "Robin Williams's Biography," IMDb, accessed October 18, 2016, http://m.imdb.com/name/nm0000245/quotes.

4. "Michael Jackson Net Worth," *Celebrity Net Worth,* accessed October 18, 2016, http://www.celebritynetworth.com/richest-celebrities/singers/michael-jackson-net-worth/.

5. Kelley Holland, "Fighting with Your Spouse? It's Probably about This," *CNBC,* February 4, 2015, http://www.cnbc.com/2015/02/04/money-is-the-leading-cause-of-stress-in-relationships.html.

6. George Lowery, "Study Finds We Choose Money over Happiness," MedicalXpress.com, September 19, 2011, http://medicalxpress.com/news /2011-09-money-happiness.html.

7. "Dennis Rodman Net Worth," *Celebrity Net Worth*, accessed October 18, 2016, www.celebritynetworth.com/richest-athletes/nba/dennis-rodman -net-worth.

8. Melissa Chan, "Here's How Winning the Lottery Makes You Miserable," *Time*, January 12, 2016, http://time.com/4176128/powerball-jackpot -lottery-winners.

Chapter 8 Forgive Us Our Trespasses

1. David Von Drehle, "Murder, Race and Mercy," *Time*, November 23, 2015, 52.

2. Mary Nahorniak, "Families to Roof: 'May God Have Mercy on Your Soul,'" *USA Today*, June 19, 2015, http://www.usatoday.com/story/news/2015 /06/19/bond-court-dylann-roof-charleston/28991607/.

3. Von Drehle, "Murder, Race and Mercy," 50.

4. Ibid.

5. Ibid.

6. Ibid., 61.

Clayton King is founder and president of Clayton King Ministries and Crossroads Missions and Summer Camps, pastor at NewSpring Church, and professor of evangelism at Anderson University. The author of over a dozen books, King regularly speaks to tens of thousands of people all over the globe. He and his wife, Sharie, have two sons and live in South Carolina. For more information, visit www.ClaytonKing.com.

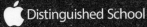

CROSSROADS *Summer Camp*

In 1996 Clayton King started Crossroads Summer Camp to provide a unique camp experience for students and leaders. At Crossroads you'll be refreshed by the message of the gospel, participate in amazing activities, worship with hundreds of other students, and be encouraged by the most relational staff in the country.

"Crossroads Summer Camp will be the best week of your summer!"
—Clayton King

Anderson University—Anderson, SC

WWW.CROSSROADSSUMMERCAMP.COM